Anonymous

Third reunion of Iowa Hornets' Nest Brigade:

2d, 7th, 8th, 12th and 14th infantry, held at Newton, Iowa, Wednesday and

Thursday, August 21 and 22, 1895

Anonymous

Third reunion of Iowa Hornets' Nest Brigade:
2d, 7th, 8th, 12th and 14th infantry, held at Newton, Iowa, Wednesday and Thursday, August 21 and 22, 1895

ISBN/EAN: 9783337732332

Printed in Europe, USA, Canada, Australia, Japan

Cover: Foto ©ninafisch / pixelio.de

More available books at **www.hansebooks.com**

THIRD REUNION

IOWA

BRIGADE.

2d, 7th, 8th, 12th and 14th Infantry.

HELD AT

NEWTON, IOWA,

Wednesday and Thursday,

August 21 and 22,

1895.

NEWTON, IA.
RECORD PRINT,
1896.

Officers:

PRESIDENT:
Col. W. T. SHAW, Anamosa, Iowa.

VICE-PRESIDENTS:
G. L. GODFREY, Second Iowa, Des Moines, Iowa.
S. M'MAHON, Seventh Iowa, Ottumwa, Iowa.
J. C. KENNON, Eighth Iowa, Van Horn, Iowa.
R. P. CLARKSON, Twelfth Iowa, Des Moines, Iowa.
S. M. CHAPMAN, Fourteenth Iowa, Plattsmouth, Neb.

SECRETARY:
R. L. TURNER, Eighth Iowa, Oskaloosa, Iowa.

TREASURER:
V. P. TWOMBLY, Second Iowa, Des Moines, Iowa.

Programme.

Wednesday, August 21st.

Reveille. Brigade headquarters and morning gun.
The forenoon will be devoted to reception of guests at trains by military escort, Co. "L," 2nd Regt., and Band Concert at Court House Park by Brigade Drum Corps and Knights Templar Band.
Dinner from 12 M. till 2 P. M.
Assembly at Court House Park at 2 P. M. (sharp)
Form line and march to Opera House.
Invocation,...Rev. E. J. Rice.
SONG, "AMERICA."
Presentation, or Introduction of Brigade to Mayor and City Council, Grand Army and Citizens..........................Robert Burns.
Address of Welcome........................by Mayor A. K. Lufkin.
Address of Welcome for Grand Army................by Col. Meyer.
SONG OF WELCOME.
Response to Address of Welcome by Col. Shaw, for Brig. and 14th Ia.
MUSIC.
Response to Adr's of Welcome for 2nd Ia., Capt. C. H. McNeil, Sioux City.
MUSIC.
Resp'ns to Adr's of Welcome for 7th Ia., Maj. S. M'Mahon, Ottumwa.
MUSIC.
Resp'ns to Adr's of Welcome for 8th Ia., Col. W. B. Bell, Washington, Iowa.
MUSIC.
Response to Address of Welcome for 12th Ia., Capt. T. B. Edgington, Memphis, Tenn.
MUSIC AND SONG.
Address, "Was Shiloh a Surprise?" Judge Robt. Ryan, Lincoln, Neb.
Song and Martial Music by Drum Corps.

❦ ❦ ❦

CAMP FIRE.

Wednesday Evening, August 21st, 7:30 P. M.

Assembly at Brig. Headquarters for Camp Fire; march to Opera House.
Thanksgiving......................................Rev. E. C. Brooks.
Song......................................."Rally 'round the Flag."
MUSIC.
"Ten Minutes with the Old Boys," Col. S. A. Moore, 2d Ia., Bloomfield.
MUSIC.
"Shiloh,"................Capt. J. B. Morrison, 7th Ia., Fort Madison.
MUSIC.
Recitation, "Shiloh's Field by Night,"................Cora M. Patten.
MUSIC.
"The Union Brigade,".......Capt. E. B. Soper, 12th Ia., Emmetsburg.
MUSIC.
War Reminiscences............Capt. Dan Matson, 14th Ia., Kossuth.
MUSIC.
"Iowa at Peace and in War,"..............Gen. F. M. Drake, of Iowa.
MUSIC.

WEDNESDAY'S PROCEEDINGS.

During the forenoon of the 21st, Garrett G. A. R. Post, No. 16, waited at the several trains and as the comrades arrived, escorted them to the court house, which was made general headquarters. Each regiment had its clerks, and they were kept busy registering names.

General hand shaking was the order. The comrades were then escorted to entertainment headquarters in charge of Col. W. R. Manning, Mrs. S. S. Patterson and Mrs. O. C. Meredith, where the assignments were made.

The following are some of the inscriptions on the wall of the the court room:

"Here's Your Mule." "1862. Shiloh and War." "1895. Peace and Reunion." "Grab a Root." "Pull the Latch String." "Our Chickens Roost Low." "Abide With Me." "If You Don't See What You Want, Ask For It."

The Brigade assembled at headquarters and escorted by the band, marched to the opera house.

The opera house was very artistically decorated with flags, banners, Grand Army badges and emblems, bunting and the like. Large scrolls containing the outline history of each regiment hung on the walls. A cannon was placed on the left side and a group of stacked arms on the right side of the stage. The pictures of prominent generals were also hung on the walls.

The meeting was called to order by Rob't. Burns, a member of the 7th Iowa, and a resident of Newton, who presided at the meeting.

After a fervent invocation by Rev. E. J. Rice, some forty little girls, all dressed in dainty white, came trooping on the stage, accompanied by two diminutive knights, and sang "America" and "Star Spangled Banner" in such an inspiring and musical fashion that the audience cheered vociferously, at both the songs and the beautiful sight presented.

The following was the graceful introduction of the chairman, Rob't. Burns, to the citizens of Newton:

Mr. Mayor, members of the city council and citizens of Newton: when the stranger is within your gates it is but natural that you enquire, and it is possibly right that you should know, who is he?— from whence came he? what is his character and reputation? what are his intentions and purposes?—are they peaceful or are they hostile? These questions we naturally would like to have answered, but courtesy to an invited guest forbids our asking them.

But friends and citizens of Newton, it affords me great pleasure and satisfaction to be able to testify in behalf of the strangers within your gates today, having had the pleasure of their company and acquaintance for the three years that I had the honor to carry a musket for Uncle Sam. I feel that I am a competent witness. "Who are they?" They are a part of the rear guard of that gallant army, that when the lightning flashed from embrasures of Fort Moultrie and sent an electric thrill through the nervous fabric of the loyal and patriotic North, left the plows, the machine shops, the yard stick and school room, and donning the accoutrements of warfare, faced southward with a firm and decided purpose—to preserve to posterity what the fathers had won. They are the boys whose gallantry and sacrifice at their maiden battle—Belmont— challenged the admiration of the nation and shrouded in grief many northern homes.

They are the boys who under the lead of the gallant Tuttle led the charge at Donelson over the abattis and frozen snow, compelling compliance with that famous order "No terms other than an unconditional and immediate surrender can be accepted." They are the boys from the ever memorable contest at Shiloh, whose commencement was on the Sabbath morning, April 6, 1862, but whose ending is not yet. But their warfare is over: the scenes of strife and conflict are long since past and remain only as a memory.

They assemble here today as your guests in peaceful years. Not the young, hopeful youths of thirty-four years ago, but as old men who have passed life's meridian, with furrowed cheeks and hoary hair long since and prematurely blossomed for the grave and on weary feet are treading that western incline that reaches down where the mourning waters wash upon the sands of the unknown shore.

This my friends is in brief a partial history of the part taken in the late war by the friends who are with us today and for them I bespeak your kind hospitality, never fearing for a moment that it will not be freely extended.

Mayor A. K. Lufkin gave the following eloquent and cordial address of welcome:

Gentlemen: That you are welcome goes without saying. That we are most happy to have you here, judge by our hospitality. Had the keys of our City not long since been lost in the shuffle of opening our gates to others, we should be pleased to present them to you. There is no assembly of men toward which the citizens of Newton feel more kindly, of which they are more proud, or more anxious to please, than the famous Hornets' Nest Brigade composed of the 2d, 7th, 8th, 12th and 14th Regiments Iowa Infantry. Some one has said that "when you cannot entertain your guests let them entertain you." So if you find we are not doing the proper thing, wade in, and we shall expect excellent treatment at your hands. The City is yours, and if the Comrades do not give you all you desire report them, and by the "Powers that be," the confines of the Guard House shall be tame, in comparison with their punishment!

Gentlemen, the intense interest for you and your splendid exhibition of heroism, can only be *fully* realized by those who have steeled their nerves for the hottest actions in the war of the Rebellion. But there is within the soul of every loyal citizen, whether or not he has heard the sound of cannon in conflict, that which dictates his readiness to defend his country, which dictates that loyalty and patriotism which is the incentive to raise up armies and navies to protect the honor, the homes, the wealth of a Nation, and were this not true, there would have been no Hornets' Nest Brigade. Just in proportion as this feeling of loyalty and patriotism is intense, can we, the younger generation, realize and appreciate your bravery, courage, strength and noble purpose. There is the same feeling of loyalty to-day on the part of the old and young, there are mother's, sisters' and lovers' hearts to break the same as then, there is the same pride and heroism to be developed, and it needs only the electric spark of challenge to all that is near and dear to us, to call it forth. But gentlemen, pardon us if we say, no thank you, none of that in ours if you please, for the capture of the Hornets' Nest Brigade called forth a hotter conflict than the taking of a nest of those little creatures whose "stock in trade" is a "business end." What boy has not experienced it! I am cognizant of the fact that history chronicles the actions of no set of men who were in a more isolated position, who ever fought harder against greater odds, and stood their grounds longer than did the Hornets' Nest Brigade. No wonder the rebel commander said that hornets' nest must be taken, the execution they were doing! But wait, wait! take it if you can; and for eight long hours they threw all the forces they could spare upon this little number, met repulse after repulse; they flanked, they raked, they stormed, but still it stood, and it was not until the day was well nigh drawing to a close, that this Hornets' Nest, indicative of bravery, was forced to yield. You meet today, dear old defenders of right, liberty and loyalty, to talk of war times and of the past, and in a jolly mood, but if Ridpath had the power to paint with his pen as vividly as could Michael Angelo and Leonardo De Vinci with their brushes, a word picture of the agonies, the torture, the terrible butchery of that day, what a representation of horror we would have! The battle of Shiloh or Pittsburg Landing, was fought April 6th and 7th, 1862. Under General Grant were about thirty-two thousand Union soldiers, and General Albert Sidney Johnson commanded the Confederate forces of about forty-five thousand men. The divisions of the Union army on the morning of the 6th were under Generals Hurlbut, Prentiss, W. H. L. Wallace, McClernand and Sherman, respectively. Early in the action the army was driven back. The Hornets' Nest Brigade later in the day held an advanced position and were surrounded but only taken after the hardest fighting. "Probably no single battle," says Sherman, "gave rise to such wild and damaging reports as that of Shiloh." On the night of the 6th re-enforcements were received by the Union army, and the next day the rebels were driven back and off the field, leaving the blue coats in full possession. But the false reports had gone forth, and had it not been for the splendid generalship, and the bravery shown by our men, on the day of the 6th, of which the Hornets' Nest Brigade is an excellent example, the misunderstandings might have been greater. The war is over and many are the deeds of greatness recorded. The war is over and many a deed of bravery chronicled, but the history of the War of the Rebellion would not be complete with the actions of the Hornets' Nest Brigade left out. Its memory will stand until lips are dust, and until that other grand example of heroism is also forgotten. I refer to the deeds of the loyal women of our land: patient, suffering, true-hearted women: doing, loving, acting on the tender side of life and being a greater incentive to battle than fear of prison, or gain of prize. Should the scene of quietude and peace be changed again to conflict you would find these tender souls ever on the helping side—

"And if Peace, whose snow white pennons,
  Brood over our land today,
Should ever again go from us,
  (God grant she may ever stay)
Should our Nation call in its peril,
  For 'Six Hundred Thousand more'
The loyal women would hear her,
  And send you out as before.

"We would bring out the treasured knapsack,
  We would take the sword from the wall,
And hushing our own heart's pleadings,
  Hear only the Country's call,
And next to our God, is our Nation;
  And we cherish the honored name.
Of the bravest of all brave armies,
  Who fought for that Nation's fame."

Bravery! yes, Heroism! yes, Loyalty! yes, all, all that was indicative of right, honor and protection to a nation's homes was true of our officers.

"And many a private soldier,
  Who walks in his humble way,
With no sounding name or title,
  Unknown to the world today.
In the eyes of God is a hero,
  As worthy of the bays,
As any mighty General
  To whom the world gives praise."

Gentlemen, you are *doubly* welcome.

The little folks then sang "When Johnny comes marching home." After which Col. Meyer gave the following hearty welcome for the Grand Army:

In behalf of Garrett Post, No. 16, I extend to you a few words of cordial welcome.

Our Post was one of the first organized in the state, which is proof that its comrades are wide-awake, keeping fresh in memory, and are active to send down the line to the coming generations, the valor, heroism and sacrifices made during the late war to perpetuate the principles of a free government. So this welcome, at once introduces you into the companionship of comrades in full sympathy and fellowship of comrades who appreciate the services you rendered our nation on that bloody Shiloh battlefield, where you earned the significant name "The Hornets' Nest Brigade."

In addition we mention that our Post is made up of comrades engaged in all the pursuits of life, and endowed with such a stock of intelligence, that it is constantly drawn upon to fill manifold civil offices, and their integrity is such that no case has been known when there has not been a true account rendered of the trust, even to the last penny. So we tender you the assurance that the safety of your wallets is all the same in or out of your pockets. The ability of the comrades of the Post is equal to the discharge of any call into office, and there is an expectancy of some to hear the call "Come up higher," but as is often the case with those most competent, there is a diffidence mingled with the expectancy, keeping them back, such as Gen. Grant, who never would have been called to lead our armies to the final victory if it had devolved upon his own movement. Rosecrans had to lose his greatest battle, before the call came to Gen. Grant to take charge of all the Union forces. The political distresses of the country are such, that, as it seems, some of the comrades of the Post are anxiously peering forward to political defeats, awaiting to be called to lead the forlorn hope to victory, and we are sure that in such a crisis none of our Post would hesitate to heed the higher calling and assume the awful responsibility, even that of the chief executive of the foremost nation of the world. Again it has passed current for years and years that the soldiers while in the army were constantly appropriating to their own use things that did not belong to them. Our past is guiltless. There is not a single comrade that did any such thing, we emphatically repel the charge. We enlisted and went into the war to fight for righteousness, justice, liberty and freedom. It was a Holy war. It was God's cause. We fought under the stars and stripes, the banner of the Lord. To him belong the cattle of a thousand hills, which includes all the porkers, turkeys and chickens and everything else on all the hills and valleys. The Bible explicitly says that "The earth is the Lord's and the fullness thereof." In so many words it says "All things are yours, whether Paul or Apollos or Cephas, or the world, or life, or death, or things present or things to come, all are yours." Into such companionship I have the honor to invite you, to invite you, dear, surviving comrades of the world renowned Hornets' Nest Brigade.

The following responses were made to the addresses of welcome, each Regiment being represented:

Col. Shaw, Fourteenth Iowa.

Comrades of the Hornets' Nest Brigade, and of the Grand Army, and Citizens:

I thank you for the welcome that you have given me as I have been on the floor, and I thank your committee on arrangements for putting on somebody that can't make a speech, so I shan't detain you long. We feel very grateful to the citizens of this town for the splendid reception of our Brigade, so finely expressed by your men. I assure you, it is very grateful to us old soldiers to have our services recognized by the people. Nearly a third of a century since this battle occurred, but the people of the country seem just as willing to recognize our services now as they did on the day on which they heard of our success in that battle. And it will be belying every soldier here to say that he doesn't feel grateful for that recognition. It gives us pleasure to understand that we rendered a service to our country at that time, that was worthy of memory. It was worthy of being thought of and felt with gratitude by the people that have succeeded us. A whole generation has passed since the battle of Shiloh, and we that remain here are ready to pass out and give place to a succeeding generation. We believe that our memories remain green in the hearts of the people yet.

The two great battles of the war that gave the first impulse of success to the Union, were the battles of Donnelson and Shiloh. On this we have the authority of the greatest general, Sherman, and all of you who are old enough recollect the enthusiasm that day the news from the battle of Donnelson was received in the State of Iowa. Why, I could show you a special order sheet by Gen. Baker to the adjutant general of the state, and I suppose by the authority of the state, that every man in the state of Iowa was to get drunk and have the best time he could. Well, now, that was indicative, probably, of the times. The order now would be that every man should keep sober and not go to the saloons, but go to some good reunion of the soldiers—but that didn't express Gen. Baker's enthusiasm on that occasion.

Now the men of the Hornets' Nest Brigade were at that battle. The 2nd regiment that first entered the fortifications of Donnelson performed the greatest service that had been performed by any one regiment at that time. I marched up a little to the right of them and saw them falling by the hundreds and never wavering in the ranks, every man pressing forward to the object for which they had started. That regiment was in the Hornets' Nest. The 7th Iowa followed them. That regiment too was in the Hornets' Nest Brigade. The 14th marched a little to the right, abreast of them, and that regiment, too, was in the Hornet's Nest. The 12th, a little further to the left, in another brigade, but entered about the same time. So we feel that we were entitled to some gratitude from the people for our services, and we feel that those services have been recognized, which is the most grateful feeling that a person can have—to know that he has done a good service.

Now I don't mean to say anything, I don't know that I could be heard if I did say anything; old age is crowding on me. I am the only colonel left, not only in the Brigade but in the five Iowa regiments that stood at what is called the Hornets' Nest. I admit that there seems to be an impression that we did more fighting than the other fellows, and that is a mistake. I think we did about as much killing with as little hurt to ourselves as anybody on that field, as much hurt to the enemy, and that was my idea of what a soldier should be.

I have been in the Mexican war—trained under Gen. McCrea, an old Indian fighter, and I have been for five or six years on the plains, and I had an idea that a soldier was a man who hit the enemy and didn't get hit himself. Well, I admit we didn't suffer very much, and although the fighting was more heavy in front of us, charge after charge was repulsed with very little loss to ourselves. On the left of us was much heavier fighting—in Hurlbut's brigade and Lauman's brigade, two regiments at least which have a right to claim a position in the Hornets' Nest Brigade; beyond that was Williams' brigade, with the 3rd Iowa and an Illinois regiment, in the front of which Johnson put his best brigade. I might say here, that the heaviest fighting was done to the left of us and not in front of the Hornets' Nest Brigade. That we did stand there and resist every attack made upon us, and hold our ground from morning till night, is another fact, and it was largely owing to the position which we occupied—an old sunken road, and the thick timber in front of us, and which the rebels themselves designated as the Hornets' Nest. We didn't call it the Hornets' Nest. And we remained there a little too long, until we got surrounded and captured. Now I say that here—I don't want it to get out.

To some of our friends I want to say, that the government has concluded to make of the battle-field of Shiloh, a national park, and to allow us to put up monuments where we fought and where we stood that day, and some of the men want to put up a monument where they surrendered. Now some fellow will come along and read that—that we surrendered there; he won't read why we surrendered; if he did read it he wouldn't understand it, and my opinion is, we better not say anything about that surrender.

I don't know as this is a reply to our address of welcome; but I say, we are all very grateful for the manner in which we have been received, and it is all very pleasant. Some of you are not as old as I am. I think I am about the oldest here, with the exception of Gen. Prentiss. If you want to hear about the battle of Shiloh, Gen. Prentiss is the man to talk to you about that.

And by way of an apology, I had appointed Judge Chapman, of Nebraska, to take my place and reply to this address of welcome. He is not here. I appointed Doctor——————but he is not here, and now that you have been bored by my remarks, why, just lay it to the Doctor.

CAPT. C. H. McNEIL, Second Iowa, Sioux City.

Mr. President, Ladies, Gentlemen and Comrades:

It had been well had my friend Col. Ryan took the hint when I wrote him that possibly I could not be here at the opening exercises, and had appointed some one better qualified to fill the place, but he did not "tumble worth a cent." He did not let me off—here I am. I will not prolong your agony long.

The Iowa brigade, consisting of the 2nd, 7th, 8th, 12th and 14th Iowa regiments has been called the Hornets' Nest Brigade. You have heard of the part they performed at Shiloh and how the term originated. The organization was a temporary one. After Shiloh, where so many of our comrades of the 8th, 12th and 14th were made prisoners, and during the defense of Corinth, the members of these regiments were formed into a regiment and called the Union Brigade. The Iowa boys were not particularly proud of this organization; although they did not forget, they were ready and willing when called upon to do their duty; and at the first day's fight in the battle of Corinth, in October, '62, in company with the 7th and 2nd Iowa and 52nd Illinois, gave the rebels the only repulse they met that day. After the prisoners were exchanged, these regiments forming this organization were transferred to other commands, and the organization known as the Hornets' Nest Brigade terminated as a body.

Those were busy days to us, comrades. We were making history rapidly, though I do not know that any of us were hungering after the job of making history.

It has been said that the old soldiers' delight to meet and pat one another on the back and make each other believe that we are all heroes. Possibly this is so. If so, just pardon me a little. The term is a general one and we have heard it freely applied in the eloquent address of welcome by His Honor, the Mayor. All boys in blue were called heroes, and I trust the honor was deserved. But, comrades, we must not take all the credit and forget the girls in blue. Our mothers, sisters, wives and sweethearts all performed their part, and the long, weary years of the terrible struggle patiently suffered at home, hoping and praying for the end of the terrible conflict, writing long, cheerful, loving letters to the loved ones in the field, encouraging them and cheering them during the long weary hours of camp life. And, comrades, I submit, if the boys in blue are termed heroes, are not the girls in blue equally entitled to the term of "sheroes"?

Since the termination of the war, I have been unable to attend any of the reunions of the regiment, but I promise myself the pleasure of doing so in the future. It certainly is a pleasure to meet and feel the warm hand-clasp of the comrade who has marched and fought with you, shoulder to shoulder, in the struggle to preserve the Union. More than one-third of a century has passed since the battle was fought which we meet this day to commemorate. Comrades, we are all on the short side of life's journey. The new generation are fast forgetting the services rendered our country by the soldiers of the war, but, comrades, we cannot forget them; we must not forget the trials and sacrifices of 1861. Many lie sleeping in the graves of the south; thousands lie sleeping in the graves in national and private cemeteries. We still have those among us suffering from wants, exposures and privations. It is therefore meet that we should assemble to do honor to the dead and to the living hero. In behalf of the 2nd Iowa, and the cordial greeting and kind words—I thank you.

MAJ. SAMUEL M'MAHON, Seventh Iowa.

Mr. President, Chairman, Ladies and Gentlemen, and Comrades of the Brigade:

It seems to me about the best appreciation a man can feel or make to a welcome of such splendid hospitality as is presented to us today, is the effort that he makes to accept it. And I have come 300 miles to accept their hospitality today, my friends. I think, however, the last twenty miles from the trunk line of the Central railroad of Iowa, from New Sharon to Newton, was the longest half of the journey, and there is about thirty comrades that came along with me on that eventful journey, who will back me up in what I say. We investigated the town of New Sharon pretty thoroughly this morning and had plenty of time to do it; then we started out and we got to Lynnville, and we stayed at Lynnville awhile, and then the train commenced backing, backing down, and the conductor happened along and he was a hotel clerk kind of a fellow—he didn't waste any words on passengers, and I asked him: "Where are we going now, conductor, we seem to be going back." Says he, "We are going to Newton, sir, going to Newton." I couldn't quite understand it until we got back to the Junction. We got back to the Junction and then we got headed west again. Well, we jogged along and finally we got to Murphy and I knew that we were close to Newton when we got to Murphy, because Murphy reminded me of an Irishman that was in my regiment, and I knew that the reunion was approaching close. Only, his name was not Murphy. We will call him old Joe. Now old Joe belonged to the same nationality that Murphy does. Old Joe regularly got drunk, just as often as he could get enough but it took a good deal to supply him. And it was middling scarce down at the front so we didn't often have much bother with it, but one evening we were down in northern Mississippi—and we were chasing Chalmer's cavalry. Now you fellows know just what it was to chase cavalry a-foot back. (Laughter.) When we got to where Chalmer's was, he wasn't there; well, we marched about thirty miles, I think; we started about 4 or 5 o'clock in the morning and wore the boys out that day, hunting Chalmers, and every man was dead tired out when they said we might go into camp. That was an invitation to spread our blankets on the grass and get out the little tin cups on our hips here and boil some coffee and go out and forage for the rest of our supper, and some of the boys started out and that night I noticed there was an unusual stir in camp. I thought something had been discovered. I couldn't tell just what and I didn't take very much pains to inquire because I was terribly tired and I didn't think the boys would keep it up very long. But the next morning we started out bright and early again—there wa'n't any eight o'clock breakfast those days. It was get up about an hour before daylight, you know, and pick your teeth and start. And we marched about an hour or so, and every fellow was cross, and his hair was pulling and his feet were sore, and I think most of them were damning everything in sight pretty much, including the main officer, and Old Joe edged up alongside of me and he had two canteens on. Well that was very unusual, very unusual for a regiment in light marching order and it wasn't the proper thing, and I asked Joe what he was doing with so much baggage. Says he, "Captain," he whispered up in my ear, says he, "would you like a drink?" Says I, "it depends on what it is Joe." "Well," says he, "just put this canteen on you," and I put on the canteen and pretty soon I was thirsty and took a drink; says I, "Joe, where did you get this?" "Why, Captain, we went out foraging last night for our supper and the boys got to a house and they found a nagur there and he told them where there was a barrel of apple brandy buried out in the back yard and we got as many of the boys as we could find and we all filled up our canteens and I don't think there was much of the barrel left when we got through." This was all confidential; this wasn't the proper kind of intercourse between an officer and a private soldier [loud applause] but it was strictly confidential between Joe and I. "Well," says I, "Joe, how in the world did it happen that you didn't get drunk?" It happened Joe had one of these quart affairs, you know, they carried on their belts to make coffee in and it held about a pint and a half. "Well," says he, "Captain, I was very dry and I knew it wouldn't do to get drunk, and I just took and filled that full and I drank it down and I wouldn't drink any more because I was afeered I'd get drunk." Now the question with me was, how much it would take to make Joe drunk; I never found out. The poor fellow is gone now and in a better country I hope. Now this has all come up from Murphy.

Well, friends, I have had a fashion of attending these reunions, year after year, and I have grown to be very fond of them and I notice most of the boys are beginning to come out. Some of them didn't use to come out, but I see several of the boys, the familiar faces of the old army boys now showing up at these reunions, but I never took any coaxing; I was always glad to come to them, and I notice one contrast, year after year, down here in the body of the hall; I see the heads of the fellows growing a little whiter, a little whiter every year, and then I look off in the galleries and I see the beautiful, blooming faces that have come up, grown up from babies, children, since the war, and I feel as I look over these galleries, that we are assured wherever we go of a warm welcome every time. And it does me good to tell some of these old army stories to these beautiful girls to whom the war is only a memory and a matter of history, and the manly boys that come out to look down over the gray heads of the men that they have already read about in history, although the time has hardly come for that yet. That will come when we are all gone, but as the years go by, my friends, the record that these walls display today will be impressed deeper and deeper on the minds of this generation—of the generations coming and growing up, and when we reflect on it the babies and children of the war are the stalwart men of today; thirty-three years, one third of a century; why, just think of it. I don't realize it. When I come to these reunions I feel just about as young as I did when I started out at 19 years old, into the old Seventh Iowa. I don't feel quite as bright often, after a hard day's work, but it renews me, this coming here and looking over these faces and opening my heart to them, and I believe we all feel the better and the younger for it. But the work, and the actions and the privations, and the self-denials of the men of the war will be better appreciated in the next generation, even, than they are now. Did it ever occur to you what the possible result would have been had the war proved a failure? Did it ever occur to you that no further south than the line of the Missouri river, running through our beautiful sister state, would have been a line of fortifications, such as are built on the Rhine, in Europe today? Has it ever occurred to you that the railroads that have been built through Iowa since the war would have gone into fortifications no further south than the Missouri river, with two hostile nations looking across their lines of bayonets at each other? Has it ever occurred to you that out of the money that it has cost for our 14,000 school houses, it would have gone into recruiting barracks for a standing army? Has it ever occurred to you that the ten millions of school fund that Iowa pours out with a lavish hand for the education of her beautiful youth would have gone to pay the soldiery? Think of it. Think of it. Has the possible result of the failure of the war, that your bayonets helped to bring to a successful termination, ever occurred to you?

Now I started in to express the thanks of the Seventh regiment for this glorious welcome which you have given us today. I read it in the faces in the gallery rather than in the graceful words of the speakers that have preceded me. I feel it, ladies and gentlemen, and boys and girls, in my heart, and I speak for every man of the Seventh regiment, that they endorse every word I say, and I want to say to you all, God bless you for this glorious welcome.

COL. W. B. BELL, 8th Iowa.

Mr. President, Ladies and Gentlemen, and Comrades:

I feel that I am in a situation that in one sense is unfortunate, and in another sense is rather fortunate. I am fortunate to have been preceded by so many in the way of a response to our address of welcome, that has been so well done, that it leaves so little for me to say. On the other hand, I am like the boy that always liked to say his piece first because some person else that talks before him, is apt to say it and he is left without anything to say, but as I have been seated here, watching the proceedings of this happy reunion, it occurred to me, according to the notification of the program that I had for this occasion, that one matter has been overlooked. If I remember, there was a quotation at the head of the program from the highest authority, something like this: "And I will send hornets before thee which will drive out the Hivite, the Canaanite and the Hittite from before thee."

It seemed to me I might be mistaken on this, but it seemed that it was a part of the program, and as no one else has made any application or explanation in regard to it, I thought I would undertake to make a few remarks on that. It seems that it certainly is applicable to this brigade. That it was so intended. And that there was work for this brigade to do on this occasion. And I have been puzzling myself to think what part the 8th had better undertake on this occasion. I would feel loath to assign them to tackle the Canaanites for various reasons: it seems to me that the 7th Iowa would be the proper regiment to assign to that task, for the reason that the number seven is a perfect number, and if the 7th Iowa is not a perfect regiment, it comes within one of it. [Applause.]

I had about concluded that I would suggest to our boys that they had better tackle the Hittites, and I want to say to the good people of Newton, that if these Hittites have much in this world, I promise them that the 8th will have some of it before morning. You remember the context of that—that this work was not to be done all at once; for the good of that people it was to be done little by little, and I will venture to promise that on the part of the 8th, that the work they do not accomplish on this occasion, they will come back again at your request and finish up the job.

I want to say to the good people of Newton that we heartily appreciate the reception they have given us here. Col. Meyer expressed my idea when he said, the soldiers should be proud that they had taken a part in accomplishing that that was worthy, that that was appreciated by the people. And I would remind the good people of Newton, the ladies and gentlemen, that this is not local, this feeling—this feeling of gratitude on the part of the citizens here—that they delight to show forth to the soldiers of the war—that it is a national feeling, a genuine patriotism. It is a feeling that is innate in human nature, provided that we appreciate it, when it is administered on our side of the issue. The ladies on the opposite side of the contest in the late war were a power there as much and in the same proportion as the women were a power on the Union side of the issue. I want to then, return thanks here, not only in the name of the comrades that are present of the 8th, but in the name of all the soldiery of the country. We would respond and bring you hearty greetings in response to this national patriotic sentiment, and, ladies and gentlemen, if I have not sufficiently expressed our appreciation of your kindness and of your entertainment of us here, we will just remind you that actions speak louder than words and we will see you later on.

CAPT. T. B. EDGINGTON, Twelfth Iowa.

Mr. President, and Comrades of the Hornets' Nest Brigade, and Citizens of Newton:

One speaker said he had come over three hundred miles to attend this meeting. I would state to you that I have come over a thousand miles. I did not come this thousand miles to deliver you a speech but when I learned that I was expected to make a speech I well nigh turned aside and concluded I must not come. I did not believe that I could entertain you, and I do not think that I can entertain you very well now, and I think I shall make my remarks but brief. But

I feel a pride in the people of Iowa, a pride in their success as a people, and a pride in them that is well nigh akin to idolatry. I came to Iowa comparatively one of the early pioneers; I came when the larger part of your state was a wilderness, a mere playground for the whistling winds. Those places now have been filled up by settlers and your people are made up of the best elements those that were not born here were made up of the best elements from the eastern and middle states, and when I went with the balance of your people into the war, your character was not yet made, because you were a State too young at that time to have been said to have had a character. But you have a character now and if you want to know what your character is, go among the people that I live among. They were the people who were on the other side in this fight and if there are any people on the face of the globe that the confederates have an admiration for, it is the people of Iowa and the Hornets' Nest Brigade.[Applause.] Why, on the first day of this month they had a great reunion at Brighton. They invited me, not because of anything personal to myself but because I was one of that grand Hornets' Nest Brigade from the state of Iowa, and I accepted their invitation, and I came to look over their program, I found I was the first speaker on the list, and I did not go. The reason I didn't go was because I didn't want to be making any speeches. I had been to their reunions before and they had treated me in the most hospitable manner, which I ascribed somewhat and to a very large degree, because of their admiration for Iowa people.

As I said, when we went out into the war, the state of Iowa was too young to have much of a character as yet. There had been no great war in which her people had participated, and even today when you come to measure her by the ages of empires or states, why she is a young state yet, in her swaddling clothes and standing beside of the cradle in which her infancy has been reared. If you were aware of the great admiration those people have for you, you could then understand the feelings that I have to desire to be in some measure still identified with the people of Iowa, and while my home is not here, my heart is often here, and I sometimes visit you because I love to mingle with the people of Iowa.

Now as I said before, this idea of character. This grand state of Iowa has verified a character for bravery which is not excelled by any state of this Union; her people have acquired a character for hospitality that is not excelled by any state in this Union, and when you come to understand the underlying cause for this, you find that one of the great causes of it is the grandeur of her women. Now it was not my purpose to say but a few words to you, but I know that this welcome that you give us, is not to us alone, those of us that are mere survivors of the late war or survivors of the Hornets' Nest Brigade, but you wish to honor those of us that are not here, those who have fallen since the war from disease, and those who died in camp or in prison, and especially do you come here to honor those brave boys who went up to their rest by way of cannon's mouth, the minnie ball and the sword, that the nation might be free, that man might be free, and that the nation might be preserved. Now as I say, it is not thus alone, and we feel, that in a certain sense, that the fittest did not survive when you come to this matter of war—the fittest have fallen and the unfittest, as a general rule, have survived.

I noted what Col. Shaw said about our not being in the hottest of the fight and at one period of the battle I would state, that so far as the Twelfth Iowa was concerned, that during the early part of the day, in the morning, a part of our regiment was not in the hottest of the fight, but after we were surrounded and after we had about-faced to fight another enemy in our rear, then the Twelfth Iowa was in the hottest of the fight and it was there that Co. A, the company to which I belonged, had six killed and twelve wounded out of an entire number of thirty-three who were actually that day on the field, and those six were killed in what is called Hell's Hollow, if I understand terms right. I haven't talked these matters over, but if I understand our position right, Hell's Hollow is the place where we about-faced and made a fight the second time.

Now I wish to say one word more. This battle of Shiloh in which about ten thousand men bit the dust, about ten thousand killed and wounded on each side, was the bloodiest battle that had ever been fought on this continent, and in any other up to the date that it had been fought. It is said of one or two battles that are equal, so since —I have not compared notes to see whether that be true or not but I have this to say, that the confederates had planned that battle with consummate skill. It was their purpose to destroy our army under Grant before Buell could reach there with his forces, and after Grant's army was destroyed they had their own theory and leisure time to destroy the other army, and it was the conjunction of these armies that they expected to prevent by accomplishing our ruin before that. Now then, it was this Hornets' Nest Brigade, the persistent fight that it made during that day, that enabled Buell to cross and saved our army from destruction on that very day, and my opinion is, that the Hornets' Nest Brigade will go down in history beside the defenders who defended the pass of Thermopalae. And when you come to speak of the fact of our having surrendered—it is true we did surrender after we were surrounded and thrown into confusion, but it was through no fault of the Hornets' Nest Brigade, and through no want of bravery on the part of the soldiers, and through no want of skill on the part of any of our commanders.

I have talked to you longer than I had intended to talk. I want to say though one word more. These soldiers are passing away. They are the survivors of the Hornets' Nest Brigade, and they are the particular jewels of the State of Iowa. You remember that Cornelia, the mother of the Gracchi, drew to her bosom her seven surviving sons after one of them had fallen in defense of the rights of man, saying as she did so, "These are my jewels." These old one-legged men, these old gray headed men, are the jewels of the state of Iowa, and they are your pride and I am so glad that you thus delight to honor them. Again I thank you for your hospitality that you have extended to the Twelfth Iowa, and to the Hornets' Nest Brigade.

The audience then arose and sang the stirring song "While We Were Marching Through Georgia," amidst waving of hands and shouts. The most elaborate address of the day was then given by Robert Ryan, of Lincoln, Neb:—"Was Shiloh a Surprise?" It was a written production and showed great care and much thought in its preparation:

Was Shiloh a Surprise?

It is but natural that as participants, we should discuss the battle of Shiloh in the light of what we saw and did, but this very circumstance subjects us to a suspicion of being somewhat biased, and it may be, unfair in our statements. General Grant and General Sherman each denied the want of preparation for that battle charged by the officers in command of the army of the Cumberland, as well as by those in command of the Confederate forces and the issue thus joined was discussed with a vigor and directness, which a proper respect for the memory of our deceased commanders renders impossible to us. This, however does not deny the right of a fair analysis of the testimony of those distinguished officers in support of the negative of the proposition under consideration.

General Grant's first written description of the battle of Shiloh was made public in Feb., 1885—almost twenty-three years after the transactions which its author undertook to describe. In explanation of this great delay he said that "Events had occurred before the battle, and others subsequent to it; which determined me to make no report to my then chief, General Halleck, further than was contained in a letter written immediately after the battle informing that an engagement had been fought, and announcing the result." The occurrences to which General Grant referred are matters known to every person at all conversant with his career; the misunderstanding of his movements and of his plans during and after the investment of Fort Donelson. The undeserved censure with which he was visited, and his practical removal from command after the achievement of the first great success with which the Union arms had been crowned

After the battle of Shiloh, General Halleck in person took command, while General Grant, still nominally in command of his old district and army, was entirely ignored and not even permitted to see one of the reports of General Buell or his subordinates as to that battle until they were published by the War Department, long after the event. These reasons of the commanding general of the Union forces for not making an official report, without doubt justified a feeling of resentment on his part, but against whom should it have been directed? The practical result of the course pursued by Gen. Grant was to subject to misrepresentation and censure akin to that of which he complained, thousands of his faithful subordinate officers and soldiers, who had the right, confidently to look to him for vindication against the unjust aspersions under which they have suffered. He himself said in the article referred to that correct reports had been published, but these had appeared at a period long subsequent to the rebellion and after the public opinion had been erroneously formed. At such meetings as these, it is possible to correct to some extent the erroneous conceptions of events entertained by the public and no one is so directly interested as ourselves that this should be accomplished. That the mere historian is apt to be anything but discriminating is well illustrated by the statement in a school history of Barnes' Historical Series entitled "A Brief History of the United States" on page 140. This model of reckless carelessness occurs in an account of the Siege of Yorktown and is in this language: "Batteries were opened upon the city, and the vessels in the harbor fired by red hot shells." With such statements of the doings of Revolutionary fathers in mind, it is not at all surprising that the youths of this generation dare to tackle the cannon fire cracker. It is to be hoped that in these meetings no material will be turned out suitable for the manufacture of such a bit of nonsense as that above quoted.

The history of the selection of Pittsburg Landing as the base of operations has been but meagerly described by parties qualified to speak on that subject. After the surrender of Forts Henry and Donelson, it was the purpose of General Halleck to mass the forces of Generals Grant and Buell against the Confederate army at Corinth. General Sherman, with four brigades, was required to land at some point on the Tennessee river below Eastport, and make a break of the Memphis & Charleston Rail Road between Tuscumbia and Corinth. After unsuccessfully attempting to comply with his orders at points beyond Pittsburg Landing, General Sherman, on March 14th, 1862, dropped down the river with his four brigades to that landing, where he found General Hurlbut and his division. General Smith, who was acting in place of General Grant, directed General Sherman and General Hurlbut to disembark their divisions at Pittsburg Landing and take positions well back, leaving room for the whole army. General Smith did not live to report what were his designs, but to General Sherman he stated that he intended soon to come up in person and with his whole army make a lodgment on the railroad as contemplated by the orders of General Halleck. On March 18th, Gen. Hurlbut disembarked his forces and on the 19th General Sherman did likewise. Within a few days, the division of General Prentiss arrived, and, shortly afterward, it was followed, first, by the division of General McClernand, then by that of Gen. W. H. L. Wallace. All this time Gen. Smith was at Savannah suffering from the injury which within a short time caused his death. On the 13th day of March, Gen. Grant was restored to his command, according to his own statement, and yet the events above described, at least till after the landing of the divisions of Gen. Hurlbut and Gen. Sherman, were according to the statements of the general last named under the direction of Gen. Smith. Of the whereabouts of Gen. Grant from March 13th until after March 19th, we have no information either from his narrative or that of Gen. Sherman and we are equally uninformed as to the exact time when Gen. Grant actually took charge of affairs at Pittsburg Landing. It is however clear from what has already been said, that for the selection of Pittsburg Landing as the base of operations against Corinth, Gen. Smith was directly responsible, and it is equally clear, that at this landing two divisions had been disembarked on March 19th—a period of eighteen days before the battle of Shiloh. At whatever date Gen. Grant may have assumed actual command of the forces at Pittsburg Landing, it admits of no question that he adopted the choice of base made by his predecessor in accordance with which troops had been landed.

The Mobile & Ohio Rail Road crossed the Memphis & Charleston Rail Road at Corinth twenty-two miles south-westward from Pittsburg Landing. Between these points there were roads, which by the spring rains, had been rendered heavy but not impassable. At Pittsburg Landing the Tennessee river ran due north, passing along the west side of Savannah about eight miles further on in its course. If all intervening impediments to his view could have been removed, a person standing on the summit of the hill which overlooked the landing and facing westward, would have had behind him the swollen waters of the Tennessee river, and in front he would have had spread out before him an undulating expanse of country covered with timber, except as there was dotted here and there a small farm, or there were the unfenced lines of highways of which the locations were governed by the conformation of the grounds to be crossed. To his left, at a distance of about two miles, this person, if nothing intervened, and his eyes were keen enough, might have made out the place where the river received the waters of Lick creek from whence he could have traced upward the meandering course of that stream toward its source in a south-westerly direction for a distance of about five miles where it was intersected by a branch running from the south-west. To his right, at a distance of about three-fourths of a mile could have been discerned the mouth of of Snake creek from which with his eyes he could have followed that creek from the river first northward, thence, after describing a curve his ascent would have been south-westward for about three miles till he reached the mouth of Owl creek. From this point of intersection this confluent stream would have been traceable toward its sources in a direction somewhat west of due southward, for a distance of about five miles. These streams for the distances they have been traced, were on April 6, 1862, swollen with rains and for the most part skirted with their own overflow waters. Within the view supposed there was partially enclosed by the Tennessee river on the east, by Lick creek and its tributary on the south, by Snake and Owl creeks on the north and west, an irregular shaped tract, about five miles across between Lick and Owl creeks where they were farthest apart. Where these creeks made the nearest approach to each other was farther out than the above line of measurement and was beyond the Shiloh church, which was about two and one half miles from the landing. At a distance of from three to four miles from the landing, the interval was of but about two miles between the tributary of Lick creek above indicated and Owl creek, and this interval was all that was lacking to completely enclose the tract, which as has already been stated, was partially surrounded by the Tennessee river and its tributaries. It is scarcely necessary to state that from a point near the landing there was a divide which ran in the direction of Corinth between Lick creek and its tributary on the one side and Snake and Owl creeks on the other.

On the morning of April 6th 1862 there was left open to the attack of the Confederate forces only the interval above referred to, the flanks of the Union army being protected by the creeks already described. The outermost line of the Federal army reached from the bridge on Owl creek to the Lick creek ford. Its right was composed of three brigades, and the left of the fourth brigade of Gen. Sherman's division, the intervening space was held by the division commanded by General Prentiss. About half a mile behind this line was Gen. McClernand's division, and, still nearer the river, were the divisions of General Hurlbut and Gen. Smith the latter under command of Gen. W. H. L. Wallace. The distinctive features of the battle which followed have been described by Gen. Buell in language at once terse, direct, and forcible. In the magazine article entitled "Shiloh Reviewed" he said: "An army comprising 70 regiments of infantry, 20 batteries of artillery, and a sufficiency of cavalry, lay for two weeks, and more, in isolated camps, with a river in its rear, and a hostile army claimed to be superior in numbers 20 miles distant in its front, while the commander made his headquarters and passed his nights nine miles away on the opposite side of the river. It had no line of battle, no defensive works of any sort, no outposts properly speaking, to give warning or check the advance of an enemy, and no recognized head during the absence of its regular commander. On a Saturday the hostile force arrived and formed in line of battle without detection or hindrance within a mile and a half of the unguarded army, advanced upon it the next morning, penetrated its disconnected lines, assaulted its camps in front and flank, drove its disjointed members successively from position to position, capturing some and routing others in spite of much heroic individual resistance, and steadily drew near the landing and depot of its supplies in the pocket between the river and the impassable creek." In this energetic language of General Buell the facts are summarized whereon is founded the charge that Shiloh was a surprise by which were very nearly accomplished the designs of the enemy. The reports of the general officers on the Confederate side, written just afterwards, tell the same story of want of preparation as does the above quoted language of General Buell. In the account given of this battle by the President of the Confederate States the unanimous testimony of all the officers whose reports were made to his government was summarized in a clear and concise corroboration of General Buell's account of the events which preceded and attended the Easter Sunday morning attack upon the forces of General Grant. With the aid of the material at his command, the son of General Johnson, the Confederate commander, compiled an account of the same events as did President Davis with the same result as to the proposition that the surprise of the Federal force was almost complete. That this conclusion was reached in all fairness and candor is evident from the apology which William Preston Johnson offers on behalf of General Grant and which, because in some measure it seems to meet the criticism of General Buell, is reproduced as it was written. Beginning at the bottom of page 551 of the first Volume of the "Battles and Leaders of the Civil War," this apology reads as follows: "Grant has been severely criticised for his placing his army with the river at its back. But he was to take the initiative. He had the larger army, under cover, too, of his gunboats; he was expecting Buell daily; and the ground was admirable for defense. Indeed, his position was a natural stronghold. Flanked by Owl and Lick creeks, with their marshy margins, and with his front protected by a swampy valley he occupied a quadrilateral of great strength. His troops were stationed on woody heights, generally screened by heavy undergrowth and approached across boggy ravines or open fields. Each camp was a fortress in itself, and the line of retreat afforded at each step some like point to rally on. He did not fortify his camps it is true; but he was not there for attack, but for defense." Reduced to the simplest form, this apology is based upon three assumptions; first, that as General Grant intended to attack, the enemy might confidently be expected to await his pleasure in that regard; second, that if attacked, it could only be in the front; and third, if worsted there lay behind his troops advantageous positions upon which they could fall back and make successive stands in their retreat toward the river. The first of these assumptions has been the cause of the greatest military disasters recorded in history. When the fortunes of the Continental army were at their lowest ebb, the British had good cause to expect that attack would not come from that quarter, and yet, in this expectation they were cruelly disappointed by the sudden appearance from across the Delaware very early on a bitterly cold and stormy December morning of the mere skeleton of an army, which, upon every consideration of comfort and probabilities should have remained in quarters and near their warm, safe and comfortable fires. This attack was successful because it was improbable. Later than Shiloh, General Grant unexpectedly crossed the Mississippi river below Vicksburg, cut loose from his base and conducted a three weeks campaign so bold in its conception, so brilliant in its execution, and so momentous in its consequences, that thenceforward no one could doubt what a great general the war had disclosed on the Federal side. These successes were attained— the one by General Washington; the other by General Grant simply because each of those generals unexpectedly assumed the initiative.

The reliance upon the successive favorable positions for making stands, the last justification offered, within itself implied that there was properly to be considered the possibility that General Johnson's forces might advance suddenly from Corinth, and, assuming the initiative, drive the Union forces back to their several favorable positions for defense. This is a clear admission of an essential proposition under consideration, and that is, whether General Grant should have taken into account the possibility of a Confederate attack. General Sherman, while he has insisted that it was justifiable to rely upon the assumption that the Federal forces were to take the initiative, has made no mention of the favorable nature of grounds for defense at different points behind him as affording an excuse for neglecting to fortify his front. The disadvantages, in case of an attack which might have resulted from having in the rear the Tennessee river and on each flank an impassable stream, were stated by General Grant on page 123 of the second volume of his Memoirs. Speaking of an interview with President Lincoln, General Grant's language was as follows: "I should have said that in our interview, the President told me he did not want to know what I proposed to do. But he submitted a plan of campaign of his own, which he wanted me to hear, and then to do as I pleased about it. He brought out a map of Virginia, on which he had evidently marked every position occupied by the Federal and Confederate armies up to that time. He pointed out on the map two streams which empty into the Potomac, and suggested that the army might be moved in boats and landed between the mouths of these streams. We would then have the Potomac to bring our supplies, and the tributaries would protect our flanks while we moved out. I listened respectfully, but did not suggest that the same streams would protect Lee's flanks while he was shutting us up." Of a somewhat similar tendency is General Grant's description of the report made to him by General Barnard as to General Butler's forces being corked as in a bottle between the James and Appomattox rivers which is to be found on pages 151 and 152 of volume second of the above mentioned Memoirs. From these two incidents, it would seem probable that the position occupied by the Union forces and near Pittsburg Landing, was not in accordance with General Grant's theory as to what would have been a proper base from which to conduct offensive operations. However this may have been, General Grant would not abandon a position once taken by him, or a line of procedure once adopted, for, as he said of himself as a boy, "One of my superstitions had always been when I started to go anywhere, or to do anything not to turn back, or stop, until the thing intended was accomplished." That this peculiarity remained with him long after he had attained his manhood, no student of his life and character can for a single moment doubt. But, finding his army encamped where it was when he resumed command, why at some time was not the possibility of a surprise placed beyond peradventure? The front upon which an attack could be made was only about a mile and a half or two miles across. On the night of Friday, April 4, there was such a Confederate demonstration against the outlying Federal forces, that Gen. Beauregard advised the abandonment of the contemplated attack because he believed a surprise had thereby been rendered impossible. Notwithstanding this fact, there were established no outposts and, although there were but two roads by which the Confederates could advance near the Federal front, no means for finding whether an advance was in progress over either of these roads was adopted.

The Union army calmly and confidently ignored the possibility of an advance from Corinth, until early on Sunday morning, when something unusual opposite its front caused General Prentiss, of his own motion, to send out a detachment to ascertain the cause and the nature of the disturbance. This detachment opened the battle of Shiloh. For the most part the immediate front of the Federal army was covered with forest trees, yet although the divisions of General Sherman and General Hurlbut respectively had been encamped in the vicinity since March 19th, not a tree had been felled, neither had a shovelful of dirt been disturbed for purposes of defense.

General Sherman, who has been General Grant's principal witness in defense of this non-preparation, justified it in the following language found on page 229 of the first volume of his own Memoirs: "We did not fortify our camps against an attack, because we had no orders to do so and because such a course would have made our raw men timid. The position was naturally strong, with Snake creek on our right, a deep bold stream with a confluent, (Owl creek) to our right front; and Lick creek, with a similar confluent on our left, thus narrowing the space over which we could be attacked to about a mile and a half or two miles. At a later period of the war we could have rendered this position impregnable in one night, but at this time we did not do it and it may be it is well we did not." In this defense there are at least two obscure statements. Of these the first is that "we had no orders to do so." Who should have given these orders and to whom should they have been issued? By the expression "we had no orders to do so," it is probable that General Sherman meant that the division commanders had received no such instructions from General Grant. This perhaps localizes the responsibility, but it does not excuse the oversight. The ever recurring question still remains, should chevaux de frise have been improvised by the use of forest trees felled for that purpose, and should not some sort of earth embankments have been constructed? The closing sentence of the quotation just made from General Sherman's Memoirs makes it very clear that one single night's preparation would have rendered the position impregnable, but he darkens counsel with this final clause "and it may be it is well we did not." Why could it be well we did not do so? The only suggestion of a reason for this conclusion which he gave, was that though the course suggested would have made the position impregnable yet it would have made our raw men timid. As this proposition that shelter would have made our raw men timid is the only one to which attention has not already been devoted let us see what value General Sherman practically attached to securing cover for raw troops for the purpose of enabling them to hold their position. In his report to General Grant's assistant adjutant general of date April 10th, 1862, (page 237 volume I of his Memoirs) General Sherman after having described the abandonment of his original camp made use of the following language: "This was about half-past ten A. M. at which time the enemy had made a furious attack on General McClernand's whole front. He struggled most determinedly, but, finding him pressed, I moved McDowell's brigade directly against the left flank of the enemy, forced him back some distance, and then directed the men to avail themselves of every cover—trees, fallen timber, and a woody valley to our right. We held this position for four long hours, sometimes gaining and at others losing ground; General McClernand and myself acting in perfect concert and struggling to maintain this line." Not only was this position held by raw men under cover for four hours, from half-past ten A. M., that is till half-past two P. M., according to this direct statement of General Sherman, but this was followed by language, the fair import of which is, that it was held until 4 o'clock, and would have been held still longer, but for the fact that General Hurlbut had fallen back and it was necessary that General Sherman's division should take such a position as would enable it to cover a bridge, by which it was expected that the division of General Lew Wallace would arrive upon the battlefield. If the cover afforded by trees, fallen timber, and a wooded valley to its right inspired General Sherman's division with the tenacious courage which he ascribed to them, what would have been the effect upon the whole army if the felled trees with sharpened branches pointing toward the enemy, backed by intrenchments, had rendered impregnable the defensive line of the Union army? It is inconceivable that troops could be so raw that an impregnable position furnished for their protection would render them timid.

General Grant's account of the battle of Shiloh giving his reasons for failing to provide against an offensive movement on the part of the enemy, was written nearly twenty-three years after the events which he undertook to describe and to explain. Meantime he had brought the civil war to a successful close, had commanded the Federal armies through anxious reconstruction times and had filled the office of President of the United States for two terms. During all these years which ended with his second term, his mind had been occupied with planning and achieving one success after another. After his retirement from the chief magistracy of the nation, he was engaged in extensive business enterprises which, through the treachery of his partner, brought financial wreck to his cherished projects. There was during these almost twenty-three years, but little opportunity for reflection upon the situation and events attendant upon the battle of Shiloh. General Grant, on page 165 of the first volume of his Memoirs, makes the very opposite observation, that his experience since the Mexican war had taught him that things are seen plainer after the events have occurred. It is well to bear this in mind, for, doubtless unconsciously to himself, his account written so long after the battle, has suffered in its accuracy from lapse of time. General Sherman, for almost his entire account of the battle of Shiloh in his Memoirs, quoted his official report made shortly afterwards, as therefore, being the most reliable.

The excuse offered by General Grant on pages 357 and 358 of the first volume of his Memoirs, is as follows: "The criticism has often been made that the Union troops should have been intrenched at Shiloh. Up to that time the pick and spade had been but little resorted to at the West. I had, however, taken this subject under consideration soon after re-assuming command in the field, and, as already stated, my only military engineer reported unfavorably. Besides this, the troops with me, officers and men, needed discipline and drill more than they did experience with the pick, the shovel and the axe. Reinforcements were arriving almost daily, composed of troops that had been hastily thrown together into companies and regiments—

fragments of incomplete organizations, the men and officers strangers to each other. Under all these circumstances, I concluded that drill and discipline were worth more to our men than fortifications." It is with profound regret that one part of this quotation is read, and that is the expression that the troops needed discipline and drill more than they did experience with the pick, the shovel and the axe. Discipline and drill were for the purposes of education and preparation of men and officers for the performance of their duties; no one has ever urged that this was requisite with respect to the use of the pick, the shovel, and the axe. Relieving this quotation of this irrevalent antithesis, the reasons for not fortifying in advance will be, first, the pick and shovel had been but little resorted to in the west; second, a military engineer had reported unfavorably, and, third, the time could be spent more profitably in drilling than in making intrenchments. The argument that because the pick, spade, and axe had been but little resorted to, in advance of the battle of Shiloh, has little weight,for the proper course to be taken was for the determination of West Point graduates, educated long before the civil war at National expense, that they might be equipped for just such emergencies. Neither General Sherman nor General Grant failed to expatiate upon the rawness of the Federal officers and troops at that time under their command—it could therefore hardly have been expected that from this source should come the wisdom which should dictate what preparation should be made. With the lessons of experience came this wisdom, and with the approval of General Grant himself, the soldiers in the Wilderness illustrated the course of preparation which should have been made against Shiloh.

In the fifty-first chapter of his Memoirs General Grant said: "It may be as well here as elsewhere to state two things connected with all the movements of the Army of the Potomac; first, in every change of position or halt for the night, whether confronting the enemy or not, the moment arms were stacked the men intrenched themselves. For this purpose they would build up piles of logs or rails, if they could be found in their front, and dig a ditch, throwing the dirt forward on the timber. Thus the digging they did counted in making a depression to stand in, and increased the elevation in front of them. It was wonderful how quickly they could, in this way, construct defenses of considerable strength. When a halt was made with a view of assaulting the enemy, or in his presence, these would be strengthened, or their positions changed, under the direction of engineer officers." This quotation describes the precautions of a veteran army adopted by common consent in successsive operations in which, always, that army took the initiative. General Sherman's testimony, too, was that in one night the position at Shiloh could have been made impregnable. When knowledge of the ill advised attack on the night of April 4th, upon the Union outposts, came to General Beauregard, he advised that the proposed attack, then under way, should be abandoned, for, he argued, the Federal forces would be found intrenched to their eyes. The fact that a civil engineer could only find a suitable line for intrenchments farther back than the advanced encampments, and, that this line would have been subject to the disadvantage of the enemy preventing the use of the waters of the creeks on the flanks, cuts no great figure, for the intrenchments which this officer evidently had in mind were such as would withstand a prolonged attack, in which event it would be important to have access to an abundance of water. The proximity of General Lew Wallace with his division, the rapid approach of General Buell with a reinforcing army, and the facilities for obtaining other troops, as well as the impossibility of bringing forward necessary supplies from Corinth by the Confederates, precluded the possibility of any long continued attack. What was therefore needed, was not an elaborate line of intrenchments sufficient to withstand such an attack but such intrenchments as could have been quickly constructed, and which would have effectually guarded against the possibility of a surprise. As this would have taken but one night, but little time for drill and discipline would have been lost, while safety would have been insured and the battle of Shiloh avoided. The battle of Shiloh has been but little understood, or rather, to speak more accurately, has been persistently misunderstood from the standpoint of General Grant, simply because the weight of the evidence is decidedly opposed to his contention and because the excuse urged by himself and General Sherman, falls short of meeting this evidence, and of producing conviction in the mind of the thinking public. The impression has gained general acceptance that Shiloh was a surprise, and that, from its commencement until the close of the fight on the first day, the efforts of the Federal divisions, brigades, and regiments were to recover from the well sustained advantage which had accrued to the Confederate forces from their gallant and unexpected initial attack. In no later part of the war was it necessary for either General Grant or General Sherman to offer an excuse for a duty omitted, or an opportunity unimproved. If General Grant had frankly confessed that his want of proper preparation at Shiloh was attributable to over-confidence, just as he acknowledged his mistake in ordering the last charge at Vicksburg, and the final attack at Cold Harbor, his great military reputation could have suffered little diminution and the perverse refusal to understand the battle of Shiloh would no longer have existed. Between the lines, however, there crops out something of a confession in the following quotation from page 368 of the first volume of the Personal Memoirs of U. S. Grant: "Up to the battle of Shiloh I, as well as thousands of other citizens, believed that the rebellion against the Government would collapse suddenly and soon if a decisive victory could be gained over any of its armies. Donelson and Henry were such victories. An army of more than 21,000 men was captured or destroyed. Bowling Green, Columbus and Hickman, Kentucky, fell in consequence, and Clarksville and Nashville, Tennessee, the last two with an immense amount of stores, also fell into our hands. The Tennessee and Cumberland rivers from their mouths to the head of navigation were secured. But when the Confederate armies were collected, which not only attempted to hold a line further south, from Memphis to Chattanooga, Knoxville, and on to the Atlantic, but assumed the offensive, and made such a gallant effort to regain what had been lost, then, indeed, I gave up all idea of saving the Union, except by complete conquest." If the author of this language had frankly confessed that his reliance upon what he conceived must necessarily follow the fall of Forts Henry and Donelson, had prevented such precautions as, in the face of the enemy he should have adopted, and that, from this oversight there had been rendered possible such a surprise that only by the determined resistance of all the divisions of his army, had complete disaster been averted until nightfall, there would have been expressly conceded only what is the natural, if not the necessary inference to be derived from the language just quoted. His admission that the battle of Shiloh completely destroyed his belief that the defeats which had been sustained at Henry and Donelson, would work the dissolution of the Confederacy, was an admission not only of too great confidence on his part, but that, of this confidence, Shiloh was a complete rebuke. The verdict of history upon consideration of the abundant evidence available must be that Shiloh is correctly understood, and that there is still less accuracy in the charge that this battle has been most persistently misunderstood. There exists no reason why the great thinking public should wish to deceive itself in regard to this particular battle. It is fast becoming, as each of its survivors soon must be, a thing of the past. The dispassionate historian will gather his facts from insensate records which, while they may bear witness to the present existence of prejudice and self justification, can communicate none of that virus to his narrative of events. Then, and not till then, will it be fully recognized that at Shiloh while the mistake of one general imperilled the safety of the entire Federal army, the rectification was by thousands of officers and men, perhaps raw in drill and discipline, yet united in purpose and steadfast of faith in a noble cause—the preservation of the Federal Union.

General Prentiss closed the session with a few chosen remarks stirring the audience and making a happy closing to the afternoon's exercises.

Camp Fire.

The comrades assembled at brigade headquarters at 7:30 P. M. and escorted by the drum corps, marched to the opera house, which was rapidly filled to the utmost capacity; the citizens seeming to enter fully into the spirit of the occasion.

Robert Burns presided at the camp fire. After an earnest invocation by the Rev. E. C. Brooks, followed by a song, the first shot was fired by Colonel Moore, of Bloomfield. The speech was full of fun, interspersed with the serious side of a soldier's life and was enjoyed by the audience.

"TEN MINUTES WITH THE OLD BOYS."

Mr. President, Ladies and Gentlemen and Comrades:

I ought not to begin my remarks with an apology but I believe it is due this audience that I should. There was a time when I could say what I had to say to an audience, and say it the same day. But I felt the nudge of the good wife's elbow in my ribs this morning at 3 o'clock and she said: It is time for you to get up if you are going to go to Newton today, you had better start. And now when you take a man of my age, almost seventy-four years old, who is kicked out of bed in the early morning, at the early hour of three o'clock, and then getting here on a freight train after three hours delay, feeling as I do, as if I had been boiled with cabbage, you must forgive me if I do not entertain you.

I promised to try to talk ten minutes with the old boys, and when I say "the old boys" you know what I mean. I mean the fellows who have grown gray with the weight of years, the men who, in the early prime of early manhood went out, bidding farewell to everything at home, and went away to the south-land to do and dare and die for what they believed was the right. And many of them are here tonight, many of them who have grown old and it will be but a little while and I say it, I don't know that I regret it —because there is a time when the poor wearied soul seeks rest, when the poor wearied body wants rest—it will be but a little time until delicate hands, with the touch of an infant's kiss will close down the eyes of these old men, and it is for good-bye. But it will come to him as a rest, looking back over the years of his manhood and the great struggle in which he has participated, that this might be a home, a resting place for the children that were yet unborn. He will say, I have tried faithfully my duty; I have stood and looked into the face of the foe, met death a thousand times and yet never shrank from it; and then he will say, why should I shrink from it now. They will go away with the conscious reflection that the world has been some better by their having lived in it.

Now sometimes the question is asked me, why is it these old men cling together so closely? Can anybody tell you? Well, there are some things that nobody can tell anything about. I sometimes think I can tell and sometimes I am sure I don't know why it is they cling so closely together. The question was asked an Irishman one time, or he rather asked the question himself: "What is it that makes this light?" And he says, "I can't tell. I know it is what you call electricity, I know that, and I know that it makes thunder and lightning and all that, but may the divil fhly away with me if I can find out what makes this hair-pin burn in the bottle." You see these old men coming together. You see them meeting together as we are meeting this fall, everywhere, all over beautiful Iowa, grand old Iowa, the beautiful, and everywhere amid the smiles of women, the sweetness of song, and the fragrance of flowers these old men get together and have a grand and glorious time, and tell their old stories, and fight their old battles over again, and when the time for departure comes, with heart beating to heart, and hands slow to unclasp he says, good-bye, John, don't stay long—and so it is. We are meeting year by year, and this old Hornets' Nest Brigade—there is something that makes our hearts cling together. While my comrade was reading tonight his article upon the battle of Shiloh, how the mind wanders back. The old men go away back and live over the time now in shadowy past. How I remember it and how I remember of getting down into that old sunken road, and I wa'n't the only one that did it. It seemed a little bit as though we were entirely too large, so to speak, as though we could not get flat enough upon that road. I remember of having a great big man beside of me and seeing who could get the nearest into the ground I remarked to the fellow, you are a great big, strong, muscular man and I am a little bit of a fellow, and lying down upon your right and the balls are coming in that direction, they could pass directly over my body and take you about in the middle. I am not the slightest protection to you in the world, not the slightest in the world, and if you want to do the fair thing by me, Pete, now what is the reason you can't be real clever and pick up just about a half bushel of this sand in your mouth and make a battery of yourself and get over on the other side? Well, Pete suggested to me that that was not a good time to swap horses when we were crossing the stream. Now there are a great many incidents connected with our army life that are amusing. There are a great many others that touch us with tears. There are times that come over me, and I have no doubt with most of my old comrades—perhaps I am a little bit more imaginative than some others, I don't know, but I know that there are times that I could go and sit down by myself, or take a walk away off into the woodland and sit down among the green leaves and upon the grass, and reflect, go back over these old dates and call up incidents and talk to myself—but I confess that I always like to hear a nice man talk [laughter]—and talk to myself, I don't know as I ought to say this—I can talk myself to tears or I laugh like a boy. And now this some accounts to you why these old comrades get together and talk. It is astonishing to me sometimes what an amount of stuff we can think up when we commence to talk. I know a little circumstance that came to my mind to day when I was real cross too, and it was a blessed thing, perhaps, for it started me to laughing a little. I got to thinking of one of the most ridiculous things that happened in St. Louis while we were there. The story came through the newspaper one morning that there was a man found dead in the river—drowned. Well all at once the question came up: Was that any of our men? Now we must begin to look that matter up, but in looking down, we found that the name was Herman Schroeder, must be a German certainly, and I looked over the list of my men and satisfied myself it wasn't any of my men. But there happened to be a Herman Schroeder in one of the regiments, and when Herman found that he was dead, that he had been drowned, he thought he would go up and see about it. So he gets up and goes to the morgue and goes to the gentleman that was in charge and he says: "I see that Herman Schroeder is dead; I want to see him; that is me." So they brought him in and there lay the dead man and he stood back, he didn't want to go close because it alarmed him. He says: "Mister, I'd like to have you look a little bit at that man; them breeches is brown, that is mine; there is a blue coat, that is this, now, Mister, I'd like to have you look at that man's eyes, please." He looked at his eyes. "What is the color of his eyes?" "They are blue." "Thank the Lord, they are blue; if they had been black, it would have been me." Now he had wrought himself up into that state of feeling that he thought he was dead, and now, ladies and gentlemen, if you would look at one of these old gentlemen that are standing beside me and behind me, who have grown gray, it would hardly occur to you that those men were at one time in the war, absolutely so brave, I may say, willing to take the responsibility, I may say, that awful responsibility that rests upon a single suspender button while he was climbing the fence with a rooster under each arm. (Loud applause.) There were a great many little things that served to amuse us. It oft times astonished me at the ingenuity of our men. They were just like other people, and you take the restraint that is thrown upon a young man when he is in the service, the result is it is a very little while until the younger men tire and weary of that restraint and they want to get out from under it a little bit; he wants to feel that he is a man. They were the men coming from the schools and universities, our colleges and business houses and the young man from the farm, who had to control the business of this country in the future. And they would tire of the restraint yet after all they were willing to own a respectable discipline, and during the time they were under the orders of the officers they were true and faithful, but there were times if you gave him the opportunity, he would perform some wonderful feats. I remember of one of my boys who had a long, affidavit face—he would have made an excellent circuit rider in the old time days of Indiana when I used to be there and shake with the ague—that was a singular face upon that boy, but he seemed so kind of considerate when he would come to me, and I felt now, I would like to give him every opportunity to enjoy himself; and he used to want to go out into the country and not forage, no, no! but go to the houses of the farmers and get something that was different from the army rations and once in awhile I used to observe, someway, that the hind part of my tent lifted up and a nice plate of butter or something slipped in—and I couldn't tell for the life of me where it came from. Well, I let this boy go out and he got acquainted with a rebel family, very nice people, and he used to go from time to time—he was rather of a literary turn of mind, and he got acquainted with their girls—and go sky-larking around; but it so happened, the story came to me—he didn't tell me himself that one night he went back to this same house where he had been going for several days, and he had taken the lay of the land during the time and knew just how to get into the smokehouse; and sometime in the night the landlord heard a noise outside and he went out and discovered that the noise was in the smokehouse; he slipped back into the house, quietly lit his lantern, pushed the door of the smokehouse open and held up his light full in the face of this good friend of his, that had been sharing his hospitality from day to day, and there he stood with a ham in each hand. "Now look here, young man, you have come to my house from time to time, I have tried to give you the hospitality of my house, we have tried to be just as pleasant to you as possible, you have sat down to my table and shared what we had and I looked upon you as my friend, notwithstanding you were in the army, notwithstanding you were fighting against us, and now I find you with a ham in each hand, absolutely coming and stealing from me in the dead hours of the night. Why don't you talk to me?" "Well, I aint got nothing to say, that is about the amount of it." (Laughter)

Another one of those fellows just comes to my mind. Now he used to want to go out and forage, and I says to him, now you want to be very careful, very considerate toward these people; there is nothing brave at all in trampling upon people because you have the power to do so. You will go home, and you will be a manly man wherever you go—so he promised faithfully he would, but after he had been going in and out for some considerable length of time, one of my men came to me and said: "That fellow has been fooling you—he has been pulling the wool over your eyes." "Well, I wouldn't doubt it, he seems to be a pretty clever fellow. Well, what is he doing?" "Well, he is going out and bringing in whiskey." He was then out at that time and so I thought I would watch the fellow and when I saw him coming into the line, says I, "Halt, stop right there. I am satisfied that you have been playing off on me; word comes to me that you are going out of here and bringing in whiskey and selling it to these boys here. Now I want to know if that is so?" He had a coffee pot and he had gone out after milk and he just simply raised up the end of the coffee pot and poured out a little stream of milk. Says I, "that will do"- but I learned afterwards that the fellow had taken a little bit of dough and filled up the spout. (Laughter.)

Now, my comrades, I have talked to you enough. I propose now to give way to some of these gentlemen here. I want to say, it is a blessed thing for me to meet with the old boys; it is a pleasant thing for me to look into their faces, to fight these battles over again, and as I say, it will be but a few years I will be permitted to talk to you. There is something in this that reminds me of our homes, our early homes, our early boyhood homes, and if there is anything on earth that comes into the heart of an old man, it is when he goes back to his old home and lingers around the hearth-stone. The old fashioned wheel was there and mother was spinning, and the tired boy lies down upon the naked puncheon floor and sleeps the sleep of the just while mother runs out the number of cuts that was the day's work. It is a pleasant thing; it does us good; it makes us better men; it tones up the virtues and tones down the vices, and steadily, steadily guides our wayward feet, so to speak, into that path that I hope leads to a purer shrine than that simply that leads us to the shrine of manhood. Now, comrades, I want to hear something from these old friends that are behind me here. I was delighted with the remarks of my friends here. But a thought comes to me now. Perhaps a great many men cannot comprehend and grasp the terror, the absolute terror of a battle. I cannot describe it to you, I cannot do that, no. The roar of artillery, the strains of triumphant music, the shouts of joy that comes to you from the victorious army you can't realize it; I shall never be able to comprehend and grasp it. I just remember that terrible road in Shiloh. I had a man who was wounded at Ft. Donelson but had so far recovered that he thought he would be able to participate in the fight. Now at this time that the roar of the artillery was so terrific, I saw that man was suffering and suffering terribly. In this old sunken road was a little gully where the water was washed out until it was sufficiently deep to hold a man below the surface. I took that man and placed him below the surface of the ground, until his body was completely below it, with the hope that the sound of this artillery would not injure him so much, but yet it was absolutely so terrific and so great that the blood just leaped from his ears. Now you can comprehend it in a measure, somewhat.

Now, comrades, have a blessed good time tonight, and tomorrow, and go away from here resolved that you will meet together for a thousand years to come (Continued applause.)

After a solo, "My Soldier Boy," by Miss Le Ora Townsend, Captain J. B. Morrison followed with a paper entitled "Shiloh." The Captain had recently visited the battlefield and his description of the present surroundings was very interesting:

SHILOH.

In the early spring of 1862, at a time when many of the leading men and women of today were babes in arms, there was an older growth of Iowa boys who were in arms for three years, or during the war.

The great Civil war was in full blast—the army of the Potomac was making its regular weekly forward movement, interspersed with disasters and defeats, and the people of the north were wearing long faces. The slaughter at Belmont had passed; Ft. Henry had been captured on the Tennessee river; Ft. Donelson's fortified hills on the Cumberland river had been climbed, and northern confidence lifted up with the capture of that stronghold and 15,000 prisoners of war. Columbus, Kentucky, had been evacuated and Nashville, Tennessee, given up by the rebel army.

The news from the southwest was not cheering to Jeff Davis and his cabinet at Richmond. Too much territory was being lost—the invaders were getting too far south. By both threats and entreaties the rebel generals and their soldiers were called upon to defend their firesides and drive the invaders from southern soil.

An army was massed at Corinth, Mississippi, composed of the best troops and commanded by the most able generals of the south. For two months everything was being done to get ready for the most desperate fighting. It was the flower of the rebel forces in the southwest, and contained forty thousand fighting men.

While this was going on Gen. Grant was sending up the Tennessee river steamboats loaded with soldiers. They were debarked at Pittsburg Landing, Tenn., a point twenty-six miles northeast from Corinth, Mississippi. Some of these troops had seen service at Belmont, Ft. Henry and Ft. Donelson, but many were fresh from the farms and workshops of Ohio, Indiana and Illinois, had never been under fire and scarcely knew the manual of arms. They marched up the hill at Pittsburg Landing and went into camp wherever they pleased; some selecting a grove, others a hillside, and others a camp nearer a creek, so that this army of 33,000 men were scattered haphazard over several miles, and as it happened, the rawest troops were on the front line. Gen. Grant, the commander, was at Savannah, seven miles below on the opposite side of the river. The division of Gen. Lew Wallace, which was not in the fight the first day, (for some reason which is in dispute) was at Crumps Landing.

On Sunday morning, April 6th, at 5 o'clock, the rebel army from Corinth, forty thousand strong, suddenly and in full force attacked this camp. They found the men asleep in their tents or in some cases were just preparing their morning meal. This sudden onset so demoralized our front that inside of three hours fully 8000 of our men were "out of the fight" leaving the remaining 25,000 to contest the further advance of the rebels. Gen. Beauregard cheered on the already victorious army and told them he would water his horse that night in the Tennessee river or in hell.

The Iowa brigade, commanded by Gen. Tuttle—whose battle scarred veterans are assembled here tonight—were camped near the river. At 8 o'clock A. M. they were ordered to the front with eighty rounds of ammunition. Heavy firing had been heard all the morning, but was not understood, as no battle was expected. On the way to the front, panic stricken soldiers were met rushing to the rear, who said the whole earth was swarming with rebels and it was certain death to go to the front. We soon struck the enemy—he wasn't hard to find—and as we hastily formed a line of battle along an old road, we could see the closed columns of the enemy with flags flying and bayonets glistening in the morning sun. Their artillery unlimbered for action and they poured shot and shell into our lines, while their infantry charged us, and the roar of battle was like the letting loose of millions of demons.

Ten o'clock came and it seemed a day had gone by; noon came, we didn't think about dinner—one o'clock, two o'clock, three o'clock, four o'clock, each hour seeming longer than the one before, and still our line was held—not an inch of ground was yielded.

This was the Hornets' Nest. The reports of the rebel officers who said they couldn't dislodge that line, have made the spot famous. It has been in song and story and painted on canvas, and takes its place in American history as an example of bull dog tenacity never surpassed on this continent.

Shortly after 4.30 the Union lines on our right and left gave way and orders came for us to fall back. When, to our consternation, we found the rebels in heavy force on both our flanks, yelling like demons and rapidly closing their two columns together behind us— all the time pouring a hailstorm of lead into our ranks. Orders then came to save ourselves as best we could. We run the gauntlet and part of us got out—the rest were killed, wounded or captured. When we reached a position and again formed our lines, the sun was down. At this time Gen. Grant came along on foot and talked to us and urged us to stand firm and hold our line. He wasn't drunk then and didn't look like he had been.

Suddenly a column of rebel cavalry galloped into position in front of us and halted. Their line extended as far as we could see to the right and to the left. We expected a charge and formed our lines four deep with fixed bayonets—the front line kneeling. We hoped they wouldn't charge and they didn't. Darkness was coming on as they wheeled and rode away. Without dinner or supper we lay down, each man holding his gun. The constant firing of our heavy guns from the batteries near the river and on the gunboats, the shells shrieking over our heads, the arrival and deploying of Buell's army, which was going on all night, and the thoughts of our missing comrades, banished sleep from our eyes. We could hear the mournful cry of the wounded who were on the field before us, and the dismal thoughts of what the morrow might bring for us made the night most terrible. When morning came, Buell's army took the lead and we followed in reserve. The rebels fell back constantly and it was a "picnic" compared with the day before.

I have heard a theory that the taking of prisoners by rebels, Sunday afternoon, so diverted the attention of their men that an hour or more of precious time was lost, so that night came on before their victory was complete. I beg leave to advance another theory: Gen. Johnson, commander of the rebel army, was mortally wounded while mounted on his horse and leading a charge near the "Hornets' Nest." I want to picture to you tonight one of "the boys from Iowa" firing the shot which brought the leader down. The consternation at his loss and the delay incident to a change of commanders consumed that precious hour. Had Johnson lived and carried out the plans he so well begun, his victorious army would have destroyed the already shattered army of Grant, and reached the Tennessee river in time to prevent the crossing of Buell's command. Had this great disaster befallen Grant, his chances for the presidency would have been slim, indeed, and the train of events might have taken a very different course. So I say, that one shot, fired, in all probability, by an Iowa soldier, may have saved thousands of lives and millions of money. The victorious army of Johnson could have cleaned out Buell and marched north through Tennessee and Kentucky, whose citizens would have flocked to their victorious standards until he might have marched on Cincinnati with an army of an hundred thousand men and easily captured it, which course of events would have easily prolonged the war five years.

No man can boast of a greater admiration of Gen. Grant than I, but up to that date one element was lacking. He hadn't learned to dig ditches. Had he fortified his army at Shiloh the rebels would never have attacked him. The men were lying there for several weeks in idleness and the work of erecting a line of heavy trenches would have done them good. The failure to do this cost the country dear, and nearly changed the fate of the war. It taught Grant a lesson he never forgot. From that day on he never moved his army ten feet to the front without intrenching it. Shiloh was the most desperate and bloody battle which, up to that time, had been fought on American soil. This is the statement of history. Of the 73,000 men engaged on both sides, fully 20,000 were killed, wounded or captured. The valor of the American volunteer soldier was fully established and we heard no more of the boast that one rebel could lick five Yankees.

The question of whose soil was going to be invaded was settled at Shiloh. From that day on, the war in the southwest was waged on the enemy's soil, so that Shiloh is considered by many as one of the most decisive battles of the war.

I visited this battlefield last April and went over the ground with men who fought on both sides. We found the exact spot where the Hornets' Nest brigade held their line. We found the old sunken road and I located a large oak tree whose top had been shot off by a shell at the left of the 7th Iowa. After thirty-three years, bullets and shells can be found quite plentifully, and it was amusing to see the visitors picking bullets out of the fence rails and wood piles, these having been made from trees which stood at the time of the battle. The old camps have a young growth of timber on them, so they don't look natural. We mixed with the people who were present in thousands at the reunion. Some were cordial; some were not very enthusiastic about our presence, but they nearly all had relics of the battle to sell to the northern visitors. The Government has bought some two thousand acres of land where the battle was fought and is converting it into a National Park. A National Cemetery, on a beautiful eminence overlooking the river, contains the remains of many thousands of the heroes who fell at Shiloh, many being arranged in groups by regiments; but the list of those marked "unknown" was fearfully large.

Sergeant Knight, late of Company "E" 7th Iowa, whose home was at Keokuk, is in charge. The rebel dead still lie where we buried them, in the open woods, in long trenches side by side. I met a man with a spade and we stopped and talked it over. He was a rebel and had been locating the position of his regiment and had found the skeletons of three men partially uncovered. He thought they were his comrades and had given them a new burial.

Nearly one-fourth of Grant's army at Shiloh was from Iowa. Iowa boys were in the thickest and hottest of the fight. The Hornets' Nest Brigade was from Iowa. The men who stood shoulder to shoulder in those stirring times will soon be gone; their ranks are already thin—more are on the other side than remain here. While we live, let us ask Iowa to do something to mark the spot where our comrades shed their blood for the common good of all. Other states have their monuments at Gettysburg and Chicamauga, showing the spots on which their soldiers did deeds of valor. Let us resolve tonight, as citizens of Iowa, that we will see to it that our legislature appropriates a liberal sum to erect enduring shafts of marble or granite on the spot where new lustre was added to the name of Iowa by her gallant sons.

There followed one of the finest features of the evening called, "Shiloh's Field by Night," composed by Judge D. Ryan and rendered by Miss Cora Mel Patten. It was well written and Miss Patten showed great elocutionary power in the delivery. The production was based on a true pathetic incident that occurred on that memorable night. The singing of some male voices of parts of "Jesus Lover of My Soul" added force and realism to it.

SHILOH'S FIELD BY NIGHT A PICTURE. "THE HYMN OF THE HORNETS' NEST BRIGADE."

All day long the battle had raged. Night spread her broad wings over the field. Darkness ended the day's battle. The two armies, about equal in numbers, had covered the field "thick with other clay." No field in modern history can tell such a tale of carnage. No battle of the war of the Rebellion bought victory at such fearful cost.

It was Easter Day, A. D. 1862. The Army of the Tennessee on the western shore of the river, between swollen, flanking streams, had pitched their tents. The rains and clouds of yesterday had disappeared. Heaven's blue dome, pure and bright, bent above them; the sun shone out in splendor. Above the heads of that great army, birds sang their sweetest music amid the branches of the teeming forest. Trees were putting on Spring's vestments of green. Buds and blossoms, everywhere bursting into new life, fit emblems of the Resurrection Morn, laded the air with delicate, sweet perfumes.

"But hush! Hark! A deep sound strikes like a rising knell!"

Well out, and at the front 'tis heard repeated again and yet again. Who could guess that a great battle has begun? No, 'tis but artillery practice. Hark! "The heavy sound breaks in once more." This time, amid their deep intonations, is heard the rattle of musketry. Nearer and nearer upon the air is borne the "long roll" of the rattling drums and the bugle call "To arms!"

"And there was hurrying to and fro." The approaching sound of conflict told but too plainly that the surging tide of the first fierce onset was sweeping before it the Union arms. Stubbornly they held their ground. Fiercely fighting, they contested every foot of ground, falling back. Now, under arms, the whole army "to the rescue" hastened to the front. Then, "swiftly forming in the ranks of war," the tide of battle was arrested. Here, front to front, every available man of the two armies grappled in the struggle. All day through the battle raged, surging backward and forward, now losing ground, now regaining; struggling, writhing and bleeding, hilt to hilt, like two giants contending in deadly combat.

From the "morning gun" till the "evening gun" how changed! Heaven's blue dome is shut out by the smoke of battle, hanging black and low like a pall. The sun, no longer "pure and bright," has, like the field it shown upon, taken on a redder hue, wrapped in its sable and battle-smoked mantle. It sinks out of sight, as if refusing longer to witness the work of human slaughter. The songs of the birds have given place to the whistle of bullets and the screech of shells. Blossoms and flowers have taken on a deeper dye. The sturdy oaks are torn and shattered as when a tornado in its course leaves the forest rent and strewn.

Night separated the combatants. The armies, exhausted and bleeding, withdrew to bivouac on the "gory beds" till the morrow's sun would light them again to battle.

Between the lines, mingled one with another, lay thousands of killed or wounded, here one in blue, there one in gray.

Night drew on. Oh, that long and dreary night! Oh, that night of horrors! From the gaping and bleeding wounds of thousands, the unstaunched life-blood was ebbing in blackest darkness. With none near but those disabled or cold in death, the wounded lay all night on that horrid field.

The noise of battle had given place to the confused sounds of bivouacing armies, seeking position for a night's repose, doubtless the morrow's line of battle.

The night was well spent ere the armies slept. Hushed was the roar of battle and, in its stead, cries of the wounded were heard, broken only by the loud roar from the gunboats, whose shrieking shells at short but regular intervals all night long were hurled upon that field. The aim of the guns was directed, as well as might be, at the lines of the bivouacing enemy; but, with seemingly fateful certainty, they fell among the helpless wounded on the field.

But hark! what is that new sound that breaks in on the ear? Is it the sounds of awakening guns, or do reinforcements signal to us— or to them? Ah! see the red lightning "painting wrath on the sky," and hear the loud thunder resound! It is as if Heaven's batteries replied to earth's feeble ordnance. Quick flashes scarce divide the loud peals of thunder. The storm, full of wrath, bursts with sudden fury, making blacker still, but for the lightning, the blackness of that black night.

When the night was well advanced, before the storm came on, out beyond and in front of the position held during the day by "The Hornets' Nest Brigade," and where the carnage was the thickest on that field, a voice was heard singing. Striking contrast! Strange place! Sweet voice! Dear soul! Hark!

> "Jesus, lover of my soul,
> Let me to thy bosom fly!"

With this strain the voice ceased, as if the last expiring breath were expended in a dying effort. What to him now was yesterday's battle! What of to-morrow's dread conflict to come!

> "He has slept his last sleep, he has fought his last battle.
> No sound can awake him to glory again."

Short was the interval before the same inspiration, that lifted the singer above the field of battle to other realms, was caught up and this time two voices were heard:

> "Jesus lover of my soul,
> Let me to thy bosom fly!
> While the nearer waters roll.
> While the tempest still is high!"

With the bursting of the storm, and while the tempest still was high, the song ceased. At length the storm spent its fury and was gone; but the wounded soldiers, now drenched with the rain that had cooled their fevered flesh, were still there. With the disappearing storm again arose from that field of the dead and the dying the sweet melody—this time sung by a chorus of voices:

> "Jesus, lover of my soul,
> Let me to thy bosom fly!
> While the nearer waters roll,
> While the tempest still is high.
> Hide me, Oh! my Savior, hide,
> Till the storm of life is past,
> Safe into the haven guide,
> Oh, receive my soul at last!
>
> "Other refuge have I none
> Hangs my helpless soul on thee.
> Leave, Oh, leave me not alone,
> Still support and comfort me!
> All my trust on thee is stayed,
> All my help from thee I bring,
> Cover my defenseless head
> With the shadow of thy wing!"

The soldiers of the North and the soldiers of the South—their voices blended! There went up from that battle-field the sure promise of a glorious Union—one religion, one kindred, one country, one flag!

When morning came, some of those voices were hushed. In the darkness of night the icy finger of death had touched the parched lips, and tongues that had sung so sweetly the night before were forever still! The refuge of which they had sung had been attained! Others were rescued by comrades who in yesterday's battle had fiercely, savagely fought, but who now, with touch as tender and gentle as that of a loving mother, bound up the wounds and ministered to the wants of comrades. Possibly some who sung there that night are here to join hands and voices with us now. This hymn is, and of right ought to be, "The Hymn of the Hornets' Nest Brigade."

After a solo, "Tender and True," sung by Mrs. Ella Eberhart, came a well written and interesting paper by Capt. E. B. Soper,

12th Ia. that was especially interesting to those who belonged to what was called the Union Brigade, comprising members of the several Regiments who were not taken prisoners at Shiloh, and were formed into one Regiment. This also being the first public recognition of the Brigade by an address given at any of our reunions:

THE UNION BRIGADE.

The 12th Iowa was camped near the river bank, below the landing, on a high bluff, over-looking the river. When the Regiment went out to the fight on Sunday morning, there were left in camp only the convalescents, who were unable to don their accoutrements and march out to the fight; and all who went out with the Regiment were either killed, wounded or taken prisoners. That news of the fate of their comrades only reached those in camp the second day of the battle and when the rebels were driven off the field, squads of each company who were able to walk, under the leadership of N. G. Price, of Company D, who had by a ruse escaped after capture by the enemy, sought the bodies of their comrades and bunk-mates among the killed on the battlefield, and wounded comrades among the multitude brought to the landing by the ambulance corps. Such search was continued until the bodies of all those, who from the reports of the wounded, were known to have been killed, were found, and given a soldier's burial on a point of the bluff over-looking the river, with headboards to their graves, upon which was inscribed their name, company, regiment and cause of death.

After the dead were buried and the wounded, who were found on the battlefield or who escaped from the enemy during their removal from the battlefield toward Corinth, had been cared for and sent away on hospital boats, those remaining made the best of their situation and surroundings, and lived at ease and in comfort in the camp until the 27th of April, 1862, when there came from division headquarters a general order creating an aggregation designated as the Union Brigade, composed of the remnants of the captured regiments, namely: the 8th, 12th and 14th Iowa and 58th Illinois, organizing them into companies and designating their commanders. As the 12th had more men taken prisoners at Shiloh than any other regiment, it had much fewer men than any of the other regiments; consequently, the 12th was formed into one company and the others into three companies each; the 12th Iowa constituted company E, of the Union Brigade, as it organized. Each of the ten companies constituting the brigade was officered by a commissioned officer acting as captain, and commissioned or non-commissioned officers acting as lieutenants; no field officers in any of the four regiments were present for duty, and Captain Healy of the 58th Illinois was designated as acting colonel. Capt. Fowler of the 12th Iowa was acting lieutenant colonel, and Captain Kittle of the 58th Illinois was acting major.

The organization was perfected, (not, however, without "kicking"), and the unnecessary baggage, tents and camp equippage turned over to the Quartermaster department, and on the 29th day of April, 1862, the Union Brigade for the first time, fell into line, accordingly as it had been constituted by the order, and, with the balance of the 1st Division, broke camp, and moved forward over the battlefield, past Shiloh church, toward Corinth, forming the advance line of the Federal army.

The appearance of the battlefield, with its acres upon acres of dense under-growth absolutely mowed by minie balls, and trees and saplings girdled, and large trees trimmed of their limbs by cannon balls, showing where the tremendous fighting had taken place, was observed and commented upon.

The advance on Corinth was constantly contested. Every advance was made in line of battle, preceded by a strong line of skirmishers. When the popping on the skirmish line got hot, lines were dressed up at favorable positions and a strong line of rifle pits speedily constructed, every other man holding two guns and his file mate industriously using the shovel or ax, relieving each other every minute or two. The roar of musketry on the skirmish line did much toward hastening the work. Soldiers who had shown every evidence of being constitutionally tired were frequently seen working with the utmost energy and vigor.

The advance line was constructed under circumstances above described on the evening of the 29th of April, 1862. On the 30th, the whole army was mustered for pay, except the Union Brigade, whose rolls were not yet made out; as each of the ten companies in each of the four regiments included in the organization had to be mustered separately, and as many of the companies had no officers or non-commissioned officers competent to do the work, there was considerable delay. The writer describes making out the rolls of his own and two other companies of the 12th Iowa, with a cracker box for a table, a pocket ink stand and a borrowed pen, under the shade of a tall oak tree, in the open air. As all the men belonging to the company had to be carried on the rolls, whether present or absent, and the dead, the sick, the wounded and the missing accounted for, and three copies of each roll made, the task was not a light one, but was finally accomplished and the regiment mustered for pay.

For thirty days, the advance on Corinth continued; some days our lines being thrown forward a mile or two, and sometimes remaining two or three days in one place, but always well fortified. Frequently we stood or sat all day under arms, and customarily slept with our belts and cartridge boxes on, our guns by our side and not infrequently in the trenches.

On the 29th of May, 1862, our lines were within half a mile of the rebel trenches around Corinth. During that night, unusual noises were heard by the pickets, followed near morning by a series of explosions. At daylight, our pickets advanced and the rebel lines were found deserted. A pursuit followed; the retreating Confederates passed south down the Mobile & Ohio Railroad; the Union Brigade followed, passing through Danville and Rienzi to Booneville, Mississippi, but returned to camp about three miles south of Corinth, on the Mobile & Ohio road where the entire Brigade remained until about the 15th of August, 1862, when the Union Brigade was sent to Danville, Mississippi, the first station south of Corinth and about ten miles distant. The two months spent at camp Montgomery were destitute of exciting incident; no drill or other duty from eight a. m. to six p. m., but as it was our first summer south, the heat was very oppressive, and the days were spent in the shade of the large oak trees which abounded in the camp; each individual amusing himself according to his taste and inclinations. Every few days, squads of convalescents arrived from Northern hospitals and by the time we left camp Montgomery, all those wounded at Shiloh, who were ever after fit for duty, as well as those who had been left at St. Louis, sick or had been sent away from Pittsburg Landing, returned to the command, swelling the number of the 12th Iowa present for duty, to about one hundred and fifty men. One of the other regiments whose numbers had been diminishing was consolidated into two companies, and the 12th re-organized into two companies and thereafter constituted during the remainder of the life of that organization, companies E and K, of the Union Brigade.

When in August, 1862, the forces of Price and Van Dorn began to concentrate in Mississippi, the Union forces were posted at convenient points to meet and watch their movements; the Union Brigade was sent to Danville, where under command of Lieut. Col. Coulter, of the 12th Iowa, it remained until the 1st of October. The principal employment of the command while at Danville was foraging and doing guard duty, the daily detail for which was one hundred and twenty-five men. Fresh meats, vegetables and fruits were abundant, and many of the boys here saw for the first time growing peanuts and persimmons. While the men came on guard every three or four days, yet the weather was fine, living good, and it is doubtful whether in our whole army experience a more enjoyable six weeks were passed than those spent at Danville.

About the time of, and subsequent to the battle of Iuka, occasional shots were exchanged between the pickets and the rebel cavalry, but no attack upon us was made, although of course we remained in a constant state of readiness.

On the 2nd day of October, orders came to break camp and abandon the post, and on the same evening we withdrew towards Corinth, across the Tuscumbia river, where we halted for the night, and the next morning, after destroying the bridge over the stream, resumed our march, reaching Corinth in the afternoon, after a very hard and fatiguing march over dusty roads, without water, upon one of the hottest days of the season, and were ordered out on the Chewalla road to take our places with our brigade. We formed a part of the First Brigade, commanded by General Hackleman, of Indiana, the Second Division commanded by Gen. J. E. Davies, Army of the Tennessee.

About a mile out from Corinth we met the Division retiring before the enemy, and re-forming the line of battle near the white house, we took our place on the extreme left of our Brigade, a little to the north and west of the town, between the two railroads that crossed each other at that point, and throwing ourselves on the ground, we rested, awaiting the enemy's attack. After shelling the woods in which our position was located, as long as they thought desirable, the enemy advanced in two unbroken and continuous lines of battle, extending to the right and left of us as far as we could see and flanking our extreme left. We poured volley after volley into the advancing lines with seemingly little effect, as they continued to advance, with the characteristic rebel yell; the onset was so heavy that the line broke and fell back about as fast as their legs would carry them, through the woods, into the abattis and thence at nightfall, within the fortifications, where the survivors of the command gathered. The men remained fighting behind trees and stumps, the rebel forces which made a reconnoisance received so warm a reception they did not advance. There was some desultory fighting, but no serious attack was made that evening. That night hardtack and raw onions were distributed with raw bacon, and a hearty meal made, after which, stretched upon the earth beside the loaded rifles, with cartridge boxes for a pillow, the clear sky for a covering, a dreamless sleep restored the exhausted soldiers. During the night, dispositions were made for the coming battle and positions assigned the several commands. About four o'clock the Union Brigade was aroused and marched to its new position further to the right, and near where the road from Pittsburg Landing entered the town. Here the Union Brigade lay in line of battle, awaiting the approach of the enemy.

Finally, about nine or ten o'clock, the heavy guns from Fort Robinett opened fire; we then knew that the enemy were advancing to the assault. Soon the forts and their surroundings were enveloped in white smoke, and in our front the lines of gray appeared advancing from the woods; with breathless expectation, we watched them slowly approach; to the right and to the left of us, as we were in an angle of the line and near to the town, firing began, when the rebels sprang forward to the charge with the rebel yell, and the whole Union front became a line of fire; still the enemy pressed forward, until within a few yards of our front, when our line gave way; the color bearer fell; another seized and held aloft the standard of the Union Brigade, only to fall; Orderly Sergt. John D. Cole, Company B, acting Sergt. Major, Union Brigade, seized the flag and planted it in front of the now rallying lines, only to fall, shot through the lungs, when private Isaac G. Clark, of Company D, rescued and waved aloft the flag, which he proudly carried forward as the line advanced and moved forward in pursuit of the now retiring foe. This repulse ended the battle, and in the afternoon our forces moved in pursuit of the enemy. In the two days' fight, the Union Brigade was badly punished. Of not more than four hundred men engaged, eight were killed on the field, eighty-six wounded, of whom a number died, and eighteen were reported missing, many of whom were killed or died of wounds in rebel hands. The two Companies composed of the 12th Iowa had engaged in the battle at Corinth less than one hundred and fifty men, but sustained a loss of three killed, four mortally wounded and four commissioned officers and 20 enlisted men wounded, ten of whom so severely as to have been discharged on account of such wounds; among them 1st Lieut. David B. Henderson, afterwards Colonel 16th Iowa and Lieut. A. L. Palmer.

While the troops were absent in pursuit of the retreating forces of Price and Van Dorn, the baggage and convalescents were ordered into camp on the old site at camp Montgomery, and the Union Brigade occupied its old grounds. Two days after, an attack was made on the camp by a very considerable force of rebel cavalry, but as a large number of the Union Brigade had not joined in the pursuit of Price, they were ready to fight, and did so. The enemy found it much better protected than they had supposed, and beat a hasty retreat, leaving several men and horses shot down. That evening orders were received to remove the camp within the fortifications, which was done, and when the pursuit of Price and Van Dorn was abandoned, the Second Division returned to Corinth as its garrison, where the Union Brigade remained during the remainder of its existence, doing picket duty and working on the entrenchments, a new and less extensive line of works having been laid out after the battle, which, however, included the principal forts. As our comrades who had been taken prisoners at Shiloh were paroled in October, we were anxious to get north, and finally after long and impatient waiting, an order came on the 17th of December, 1862, dissolving the Union Brigade and ordering its return home to join the exchanged prisoners and re-organize their old regiments, and on the 18th of December, with light hearts and thoughts of a merry Christmas at home, the 12th Iowa, under command of Lieut. Col. Coulter, gaily marched to the depot and boarded the cars for the north. Arriving at Jackson, Tennessee, about eleven A. M., we found consternation and commotion. Forrest was on a raid. North of Jackson the telegraph lines were cut and an attack was hourly expected. We were ordered to disembark and assist in the defense of the post. That night the track was torn up and bridges burned almost to as far north as Columbus, Kentucky. The disappointment was keen, but there was no help for it, and we climbed down and loaded our guns, and were assigned an exposed position on the picket line. No attack came. After waiting impatiently for three days, we were allowed to go north as guard for the engineer corps and construction train, to rebuild the bridges and track which the rebels had destroyed. For two weeks and over we moved along with the bridge gang, from stream to stream, across the swamps, counting the miles, even the ties, as so much nearer home; sleeping behind anything that broke the chilly wind, sheltered only by our blankets and overcoats. The country through which we passed was composed mostly of swamp, with plenty of cane brakes and thinly populated. We lived off the country. Sometimes foraging was good; sometimes not so good; we ate what we could find and hoped for better with the next move. Our living varied from the milk and honey variety of some neighborhoods to roast "razor backs" in others; but taken all in all, with the adventure and the marching, the bridge building and the picket duty and interviews with the natives, we did not have such a bad time. In fact, if we had not been so anxious to get home by New Years, we would rather have enjoyed the trip. Finally, however, the last burned bridge was reached, the river hastily crossed on false work, and the boys swung out with rapid strides, up the railroad track towards Columbus and toward home. That night we slept in the deserted buildings at Union City, and the next day, January 4, 1863, marched into Columbus, and that night took a steamer for Cairo, arriving on the 5th, and the next north bound train on the Illinois Central bore us Davenportward, where we arrived the 7th of January; received from Adjt. Baker a twenty day furlough and transportation to our several homes.

After a song by the Ladies Quartette, Capt. Dan Matson, of the Fourteenth, then gave us "War Reminiscences," that called to the minds of many of the comrades several incidents that occurred during their sojourn in Dixie:

I feel more insubordinate, tonight, toward my Brigade Commander than I ever felt before. He taught me silence in the ranks when on duty, and here in gross violation of this positive training of Army Regulations, he bids me talk to this audience; and this is not all. I charge him with further violation of Regulations, in that he orders me into action, placing me under a severe cross fire, without furnishing me ammunition; and, too, the treasured haversack with its three days rations; and the old canteens are missing. *Unarmed! rationless! under fire! and the old chief in the rear!* Boys, it aint like it used to be; you know he once told us that he never put us in tough places without being himself *in the lead*, and we threw it back at him. *Old man, we never went out until you took us out.*

Dr. Staples of the Fourteenth tells a story on Col. Shaw that may be new to some of you. Our first Chaplain had a wry neck and held his head to one side. His horse also had a wry neck and held his head over the opposite way. They cut quite a figure on parade occasions,

One day at Benton Barracks, the Regiment was formed for battalion drill, while the Colonel not altogether calmly, awaited the appearance of his orderly with "old Pete" his horse his mood was very much like that of Phil Sheridan, at Five Forks, when Warren and the 5th corps didn't come to time. Somebody was in danger of getting relieved. The Chaplain who was standing near by, holding his old stiff necked horse, thinking to help his Commander out of the dilemma, led old "crooked neck" up to the Colonel and meekly said: "Col., you can take my horse." There was a pause as if Nature stood trembling for the answer: the *explosion* which followed would be hard to describe; it was none of your ricochet shots; it took the old Domnie and old twist neck right amidships. Suffice it to say, the horse had to be closely blanketed for many weeks until his hair grew out again, and when Domnie arose to his feet, it was noticeable that his head was a couple of degrees more out of line. The Colonel was famous for looking out for his boys; he took good care to get us all that was coming to us, and sometimes we got things that were not exactly our due according to existing Regulations. In the early part of March, 1862, while encamped at Metal Landing on the Tennessee river after the Donelson fight awaiting transportation to Pittsburg, he concluded one day it was time the men had some fresh beef. So riding up to Brigade Headquarters, Col. Lauman, he addressed him: "Lauman, my men need some fresh beef"; "Well," says Lauman, "I haven't got any; it can't be had!" Shaw replied, "I can get it." "Well get it." said Lauman a little testily. Shaw wheeled his horse and rode back to camp and reining up before the quartermaster's tent: "Buell," he called to that official, "get on your horse and come with me." Mounting in obedience to the order, the two took the road leading from the river into the country. About two miles out they came upon a man plowing with a yoke of oxen. Stopping him, the Colonel enquired, "Old man, what do you want for those cattle?" "Don't want to sell 'em sah! Have to make my crop with them." "That is not the question," says Shaw. "What will you take for them?" "Can't sell 'em sah," was the reply. "Well," says Shaw, "if you are a Union man you will be glad to give them up for the use of the men fighting in the Union cause; if you are a rebel they ought to be taken from you. *Unhitch 'em.*" Seeing no way out of the trade, the old Tennesseean unhooked the oxen and the Col. and quartermaster drove them off. Arriving at camp a detail was quickly made, soon eight quarters of beef were hanging up to the adjacent trees. One quarter was issued to each of the seven Companies and the eighth was cut up for headquarters, field and staff, etc. Gallant old Major Broatbeck of the 12th, sat on his horse silently watching the procession his mouth watering for a slice of the juicy meat. Unable to stand it longer, he rode up to Col. Shaw, lifting his cap he said, "Col. Shaw, you is the best Col. to your men vat ish." "Sergt., cut the Major a steak and hand it to him." On securing it the Major bowed his thanks and rode away. Then Shaw directed the Sergt. to cut off a steak and send it to Brigade Headquarters with the compliments of Col. Shaw. Thus the Fourteenth obtained their first supper of beef at the expense of the Confederates; but it wasn't the last. Some months later, when we with the comrades of the 1st Brigade were boarding at the Hotel Davis in the old cotton shed at Cahaba, Alabama, our generous host one morning rolled into the pen several barrels of corned beef. We knocked in the heads, when horrors! if a ten inch shell had dropped in there sizzling it couldn't have caused a bigger scatterment. The aroma that arose from those barrels ranked Gen. Halleck- whom we all swore by those days and was stronger than Sampson that beef was tougher when we tried to cook it than the yoke that was on the cattle that Col. Shaw and Buell bought of the old Tennesseean, up at Metal Landing.

At the first charge of Gibbons Brigade on our lines at Shiloh, Comrade J. U. Guthrie of Co. K, 11th Iowa, captured the flag of one of the rebel Regiments. He only got the colors; a rebel sergeant got away with the staff. Methinks I can see brave Guthrie's beaming countenance yet, as a minute or two later he held it up to our view, saying, "See here, boys, I've got their flag!" He folded it up and placed it across his breast, buttoning his jacket over it. In this way it was carried until his capture at the close of the day, when he destroyed it.

A wounded rebel belonging to Lee's army lay a little distance from the roadside on the line of the Confederate retreat from Petersburg to Appomattox. He was terribly hurt and called most piteously for help. Along the road trudged a Yankee private belonging to the 5th corps- that immortal body of men who, under the inspiration of its commander, the Knightly Griffin, kept up with Sheridan's cavalry all through that remarkable pursuit, thereby rendering the glorious consummation possible- the Yankee boy hearing the plaintive appeal, went over to where the dying man lay. Stooping down, he said, "What can I do for you Johnnie?" "Oh, can't you give me a drink of water?" Unslinging his canteen, he placed it to the parched lips of the sufferer, who drank to his satisfaction. "What else can I do for you, Johnnie?" "I'm dying," said the injured man, "Won't you pray for me?" This was a stunner. The tender hearted fellow would do anything to alleviate the sufferings of his enemy. He would have willingly carried him in his arms if it had been any use, but *pray he couldn't*. In his distress he looked to the road for help. Seeing a squad of our soldiers passing, he called to them; and some three or four left their ranks and went to him. When they reached his side, he said to them, "Boys, here's a confed. He is dying. I've given him water, and now he asks me to pray. I can't. Won't one of you fellows pray?" One of the number was equal to the task. He said, "Boys, let us pray," and they all knelt down, while a few words were offered to the Throne on High in behalf of their dying foeman. *Friends, methinks* the Recording Angel would catch the words of that prayer and *write them in His book.*

After Mrs. T. M. Rodgers had sung that beautiful solo, "Veteran Song," Gen'l. F. M. Drake was then introduced and received a most hearty welcome. He spoke briefly as follows, on the subject "Iowa at Peace and in War":

I hardly know how to address a camp fire like this. It looks like I ought to say "ladies and gentlemen," but ladies were not soldiers during the war, but they stood behind the soldiers and sometimes I think they stood in front of the soldiers. At any rate, I don't think the rebellion would have ever been put down if it hadn't been for the assistance of the ladies.

I see that the toast from which I am to speak is "Iowa at Peace and in War." I would have a great deal to say were I to fully reply to that toast, but it is late. I am going to say but a few words. The first is to say, that I regard Iowa, proud Iowa as the greatest state in the Union, and that I am glad to know that I have grown up with it. I was on its soil before it was the state of Iowa. It was Michigan territory when I came here, and then it was Wisconsin territory, and now it is Iowa, and has been for half a century. During the war no state responded more readily and more in proportion to its population than the state of Iowa. We had much to accomplish. My first service, in 1861, the first time that I was assigned to a command during the war—I see present today, unexpectedly, General Prentiss—assigned me to command St. Joe, in 1861. I was not at the Hornets' Nest, but here is Col. Shaw that was, and my friend, Col. Moore, from the "hairy nation" Davis county. The Colonel and I lived in the "hairy nation." That is a part of Iowa, in itself. That was before the war. From 1846 until Sumpter was fired upon, Col. Moore and myself were humble citizens of the "hairy nation" and we have never been ashamed of it—are you, Colonel, ashamed of that nation? And so we have grown up.

I believe that since the war the state of Iowa has doubled its population. We have less illiteracy in the state of Iowa, and it is so pronounced and understood in the United States, and of course we put the United States against the world—I have a right to.

Now I am not going to enter into any details in regard to the war. It is sufficient to say that we had over four years of war. I know that because I served over four years myself. We had a bloody war. We were at war because we were forced to war, and for the purpose of settling the question of the great Declaration of Independence in regard to freedom. It had been said—it had been expressed—that this was a land of freedom, and yet it was not true, and it had been decreed by God Almighty himself that slavery could not be wiped out except at the price of blood, and blood was shed, and today after more than four years of bloody war, fighting our own flesh and blood, fighting our own citizens of our common country, we have a land of liberty and freedom. The only land under God's heavens that can be said is a land of liberty and freedom. It was a desperate engagement, a desperate conflict, but under God Almighty it was a grand conflict, and while the nation was in tears and in mourning, when the sunlight came out and shown upon this grand land of liberty and freedom, we all rejoiced; even amid tears we rejoiced, and today we rejoice for this great country, this land of liberty and of freedom.

I think I shall say no more; I thank you for your kind attention. (Applause.)

At the close of Gen. Drake's speech and when it was supposed the meeting was closed. Gen. Prentiss hastily arose, came forward and asked the audience to wait a moment. He then related the following incident of Gen. Drake's early boyhood:

Let us not go yet. Time makes mighty changes. It was in 1848: I was fortunate enough in those days to be a packer of pork, down at the mouth of the Des Moines river, in Missouri—made considerable money at it—and a couple of men stole a span of horses. I and another person started to catch them. It was late in the fall. We wended our way up the Des Moines valley, rapidly as we thought, trailing the team. Finally, one cold damp evening—it was just commencing to rain and hail together. We had got wet riding. We noticed a very kind hearted looking man standing in front of a cabin down near Centerville, Iowa. Riding up to the gate, there stood a youth with ragged rubber boots on who it appeared had been looking after some stock. I asked the question—could we find shelter here tonight? "We never turn strangers out such a night as this," was the response. We entered the cabin—first, our effort was to look after our horses. The boy with the boots on, a young lad, says, "Gentlemen, walk in, I will put the horses up." They were put away and in came the young man. In the night there was a terrible snow storm. There in the log cabin the snow came in between the cracks; we couldn't sleep while it was snowing. Finally, someone came lightly into the room with a heavy comfort, spread it over the pair that was lying in the bed: I was one, my friend the other; and tucking the comfort around our feet, went out gently. It was the mother of that boy with the rubber boots on, that took care of General Prentiss' horse that night, and little did he expect that man was to become Governor of Iowa.

The remarks of Gen. Prentiss caused great applause and gave a most joyous ending to the camp fire.

Programme.

Thursday, August 22nd.

Reveille and morning gun.
Foremoon devoted to business meeting of Brigade and of Regiments, and social.
Dinner from 12 M. till 2 P. M.
2:30 P. M. Assemble at Brigade headquarters.
MUSIC.
3 P. M.—Address by.........................Maj. Gen'l B. M. Prentiss
MUSIC.
4 P. M.—Form line and march to School House for exercises there under the management of Jasper County Normal. Order of March:

    1. Knights Templar Band.   6. Grand Army.
    2. Brig. Band Drum Corps.   7. Women's Relief Corps.
    3. Co. L 2nd Reg. I. N. G.   8. Ladies of the Grand Army.
    4. Firemen in Uniform.   9. Hornets' Nest Brigade.
    5. Normal School.

Exercises at the School House Grounds:
MUSIC.
Welcome to Brigade for Jasper Co. Normal.........Prof. D. M. Kelly
MUSIC.
Response } ....L. Kinkead, 8th Iowa
          ....R. M. Terrill, 12th Iowa
MUSIC.

♥ ♥ ♥
CAMP FIRE.

Thursday Evening, August 22nd, 7:45 P. M.

Assemble at Brigade headquarters and march to Opera House.
Prayer...Rev. C. C. Harrah
MUSIC.
"Johnson's Surrender to Sherman."......Col. G. L. Godfrey, 2nd Iowa, Des Moines.
MUSIC.
"The Long Roll,"......Prof. A. N. Currier, 8th Iowa, Dean of faculty, State University, Iowa City.
Recitation..Miss Belle Lambert
MUSIC.
"We took Touch of Elbows."..Wm. T. McMakin, 11th Iowa, Middleton
MUSIC.

THURSDAY'S PROCEEDINGS.

[BUSINESS MEETING.]

Newton, Iowa, August 22nd, 1895. The Brigade assembled at the Opera House at 10 a. m. for the transaction of business. The President, Col. Shaw, in the Chair. The Secretary presented the following report:

NEWTON, IOWA, August 21, 1895.

To the comrades of the Iowa Hornets' Nest Brigade, I submit the following report:

RECEIPTS:

Sept.	2, 1890,	to cash from dues			198.00
"	3,	" order No 1			8.50
"	"	" " " 2			30.25
"	"	" " " 3			5.00
"	6,	" " " 4			.10
"	"	" " " 5			8.30
July	11, 1895	" " " 6			20.75
Aug.	7,	" " " 7			2.00
	By balance due, order 8				30.21
					$201.11

EXPENDITURES.

Sept.	2, 1890,	by balance due secretary		$17.00
"	"	" 1 Bolt Ribbon		2.00
"	"	" Printing Badges		1.25
"	"	" Rent for hall		8.50
"	"	" Singing Books. Turk Moore		5.00
"	"	" Express charges on music books		.10
"	"	" Receipt, Treasurer V. P. Twombly		98.00
"	"	" Express on Pamphlets		.35
"	"	" Expense of Secretary		8.30
July	11, 1895,	" 1800 Postals and Printing		20.75
Aug.	7,	" Postage and stamps		1.55
"	13,	" Bill of Baldauf (Badges)		23.81
"	14,	" Printing Badges		2.50
"	21	" Expense and Services of Secretary		12.00
				$201.11

Our Constitution calls for a Reunion every three years, the last one was held at Des Moines Sept. 2, 1890, and this one should have been held in 1893 but the World's Fair coming that year and the hard times following, the executive committee decided, unanimously, it would be better to postpone the reunion.

At a meeting of the executive committee held in Des Moines, June 18, 1895, an invitation was extended by the citizens of Newton, through Col. Ryan to hold our reunion this fall at that place. The committee accepted the invitation and set the date for August 21 and 22, 1895.

The following comrades were elected a committee on arrangements with D Ryan as chairman:

    D. Ryan.
    V. P. Twombly, 2nd Iowa.
    R. P. Clarkson, 12th Iowa.
    Joe. McGarrah, 14th Iowa.
    Robert Burns, 7th Iowa.

At our former reunions I had sent out printed notices to the secretaries of the different regiments for distribution but I decided this time to send the notices myself. I wrote the secretaries of the different regiments for the list of their members, to which they promptly responded.

July 11th I had 1800 cards printed giving notice of our reunion. All but about 150 of which were sent to the comrades of the different regiments. Between 80 and 100 cards were sent to the newspapers throughout the state. Comrade Baer, S'cy. of the 7th Iowa, living in the same place I do kindly consented to send out the notices for his regiment for which I tender him thanks. I think by July 20 the cards were all sent. Allow me to suggest to one and all, if you would always give the regiment and company to which you belong it would aid the secretary very much; many of the comrades neglected to do this.

Another thing, always respond to any notices sent you by your secretary, promptly. Out of the large number of the notices sent less than 200 responded; only about 20 cards were returned uncalled for. So I think the greater number must have reached the comrades to whom they were sent. I think all of the secretaries will indorse me in this suggestion, that in order to perfect the roll of any regiment the comrades should reply promptly, giving name, town, county, state and company, and unless this is done no one can succeed in making a satisfactory roll for himself or others.

I desire to thank the officers of the Brigade for the kind assistance rendered me in the performance of my duties; to the secretaries of the regiments of the Brigade for their willingness to aid me and their promptness in replying to all my communications. Col. Ryan the chairman of the Committee on Arrangements, the secretary of any organization is always brought in close contact with the one having charge of any special reunions, and I can testify to the Colonel's push and energy in his endeavors to make this reunion a success. I can assure you he is a stayer from away back, no light duty for him or those around him when there is anything to do, and I thank him for his uniform kindness and help to me.

Thanks are due the following ladies for their kindness, in preparing the badges:

Mrs. McMullen, Mrs. Baer, whose husbands are members of the 7th Iowa, Mrs. Moreland, whose husband formerly belonged to the 7th Iowa, Mrs. Eddy and Mrs. Turner, the other halves belonging to the 8th Iowa, and the Misses Carrie Noble, Mattie Wagoner and Agnes Turner.

In closing I desire to thank the comrades present for their prompt response to the notices of the reunion sent, also to those who are not present but are unavoidably detained.

R. L. TURNER,
Sec't. Iowa Hornets' Nest Brigade.

The report was adopted. The treasurer, V. P. Twombly, being absent his report was read by the secretary as follows:

DES MOINES, IOWA, August 15th 1895.
V. P. Twombly, treasurer in account with Iowa Hornets' Nest Brigade.

	DR.	CR.
Sept. 2, 1890. Balance on hand this date	$15.75	
" " Received from Secretary, R. L. Turner	98.00	
Aug. 15, 1895 Received interest on balance to date	16.30	
	$130.05	
Sept. 3, 1890, Paid voucher No. 1, W. L. Davis		$ 8.50
" " " " 2. R. L. Turner, expense		20.25
" 9, " " " 3. " " for Frank Moore		5.00
" 9, " " " 4. " " express		.10
Jan. 27, 1891, " " " 5. " " expense		8.30
July 18, 1895, " " " 6. " " postals and printing		20.75
Aug. 12, " " " " 7. " " expense		20.00
" 24, " Balance on hand this date		16.85
		$130.05

Respectfully submitted.

V. P. TWOMBLY, Treas.

The report was adopted.

Col. Shaw and J. C. Kennon, of the executive committee, having examined the books and vouchers of the secretary and treasurer, made the following report:

We the undersigned, members of your Executive Committee, beg leave to report, that we have examined the books and papers of your secretary and treasurer, we find everything correct, and all moneys accounted for by the proper vouchers.

WM. T. SHAW,
J. C. KENNON.

The Brigade then proceeded to the election of officers:

Colonels W. T. Shaw and W. Bell were nominated for president. Col. Shaw receiving a majority of the votes, was declared elected as president. On motion made and seconded, the election of Col. Shaw was made unanimous.

It was moved and seconded that the present vice-presidents of the brigade be elected to fill the same positions another term; motion carried and the following were declared elected as vice-presidents of the Brigade:

2nd Iowa, G. L. GODFREY, Des Moines, Iowa.
7th Iowa, S. M'MAHON, Ottumwa, Iowa.
8th Iowa, J. C. KENNON, Van Horn, Iowa.
12th Iowa, R. P. CLARKSON, Des Moines, Iowa.
14th Iowa, S. M. CHAPMAN, Plattsmouth, Neb.

On motion made and seconded, R. L. TURNER and V. P. TWOMBLY were re-elected to fill the positions of secretary and treasurer.

Voted that the Committee on Resolutions consist of one from each regiment, and that each regiment make its own selection.

The secretary was by vote authorized to select an assistant secretary.

COL. GODFREY, chairman of Committee on Badges, stated that he had a badge in the shape of a hornet, made of metal, and to be used as a pin, which he showed to the comrades. After some discussion, it was voted to continue the Committee, and instructed them to have some metal buttons made with a hornets' nest stamped on them, similar in size to those worn by the different orders in the lapel of the coat.

Voted to reconsider the vote as to badge.

Voted to have the badge made of metal representing a hornets' nest and to be used as a pin instead of a button. Comrade Akers, of the 7th Iowa, was by vote added to the Committee on Badges. The following comprise the Badge Committee:

G. L. GODFREY, 2nd Iowa.
J. W. AKERS, 7th Iowa.
DEWITT STEARNS, 8th Iowa.
R. P. CLARKSON, 12th Iowa.
JOE MCGARRAH, 14th Iowa.

Voted to send greetings to the 30th Iowa, now holding a reunion at Brighton, Iowa.

The several regiments then presented those selected as Committee on Resolutions:

COL. MOORE, 2nd Iowa.
J. W. AKERS, 7th Iowa.
W. B. BELL, 8th Iowa.
T. B EDHNSTON, 12th Iowa.

SAMUEL CHAPMAN, 14th Iowa.

Moved and seconded that the proceedings of the reunion be published in pamphlet form. Motion carried.

COL. SHAW was by vote added to the Committee on Publication of Pamphlet.

There being no other business, the meeting adjourned.

R. L. TURNER, Secretary.

Afternoon Exercises.

The Brigade assembled at headquarters at 2:30 p. m., and headed by the drum corps, marched to the opera house, where Col. Ryan presided during the exercises. As it was ascertained that not one half of the crowd could get into the opera house, Gen. Prentiss kindly consented to speak both there and in the court yard. His speech in the opera house was a grand effort. It was a plea for more patriotism and the fire, logic, devotion to the flag, and the intense appeal to every one to be more loyal to our blood-bought country stirred the pulse and moved the hearts of the people in a wondrous way. "True Americanism" is the way he termed true patriotism. The climax of the afternoon was reached when he stepped to one side of the stage, took in his hands a beautiful silk flag, carried it to the center of the stage and called upon the vast audience to take the pledge of loyalty with him. It was a picture, indeed, to see the martial figure of that white haired war veteran standing with his hands lovingly upholding "Old Glory." After the audience had risen at his request, he solemnly repeated the vow of allegiance, and then, led by him, the men joined in three cheers that made the rafters ring, while the ladies wildly waved their handkerchiefs.

GEN. B. M. PRENTISS.

Mr. President, Ladies and Gentlemen, and Comrades of the Hornets' Nest Brigade:

To me, reunions have ceased to be a pleasure. It is true, in obedience to the request and call of friends I attend them, but memory comes untrammeled when I am at a reunion and a sad feeling arises. Not from what we have done as soldiers, more from present condition of affairs in our own country. By way of explanation let me say, I am here attending the reunion of the Iowa Brigade of the Hornets' Nest. I have but little to say of Shiloh though I claim to know much of it; I believe I was there. I have a recollection of being there, at least, and I have this to say. You have been re-unioning with a brigade that represents a position, a brigade that saved the army of the Tennessee on the 6th of April, 1862. (Applause) Those words have never been uttered by me in public before. I know whereof I speak and at my age, knowing that I am soon to pass away, knowing what I do of the conditions at that day, and of the trials, and gallant services of men upon that occasion, I can truthfully say, this regiment was located in what was called the Hornets' Nest of the battlefield of Shiloh that saved the Army of the Tennessee. I had waited for others to say that for us. But you must bear in mind the defenders of that position stood, and were captured, taken to the South and put into prison, no one to write for them whilst there. The nation being engaged in a terrible war; other battles were fought. Those at home make the report. We that were there in the South could not be heard. Every regiment had its say upon that occasion and that is what has caused so much discussion concerning Shiloh. I was pleased, yesterday, listening to the paper read by Judge Ryan. While it is true, perhaps we, some of us, might differ with him as to the propriety of discussing questions that have been discussed for thirty years. You ask me the question today in the presence of the Brigade of Iowa, known as the Hornets' Nest Brigade: "General Prentiss, was it a surprise at Shiloh?" My answer would be: No general on the Union side for one moment entertained the idea that the battle was to be fought upon the ground where it was fought. I occupied the extreme front that morning and at 5:14 the battle commenced. It commenced a mile upward and a little in front of any encampment on that battlefield, and he that intimates that any of our soldiers were found asleep in their camps and drawn from their tents to enter that battle, he is a slanderer of the soldiers that fought, that you young people might enjoy the liberty you do today.

Ladies and gentlemen, I have often been amused in visiting places, picking up pamphlets, pictorial pamphlets, in which was a picture of General Prentiss being drawn from his tent at headquarters on the field of Shiloh, by two long haired fellows and taken to the South. Today there cannot be found a publication throughout the entire southern states that has one sentence or utterance of discredit towards the man that held the Hornets' Nest of Shiloh. I visited them on the 6th of April last. I talked perhaps to eight or nine thousand of people. The Confederate soldiers were there. I was speaking of Shiloh and was very particular as to my utterances upon that occasion. I talked just as radical as I used to talk to you people of Iowa in the years past. When I was through, every thing that I said there was endorsed by north and south. They knew that we were telling the truth, and when you hear Union men taking exception to men that defended the Hornets' Nest on the field of Shiloh, put it down that they were not in that Hornets' Nest at the last hour and a half of that day. I know whereof I speak.

Ladies and Gentlemen, I am not to speak of Shiloh. I want to appeal to the young people of this country. I want to say to you that if I could have my way, the action and conduct of every old soldier would be such that you could follow his example. I am told, Mr. Chairman, you have a Normal school here, or an assembly of normal students. I would that every one of them were seated in my presence today. To you teachers of the country, let me make an appeal. In behalf of posterity, the hour has come, the day is, when we must turn over a new leaf in this land of ours. I do not enjoy the army stories at reunions. I do not enjoy the talk that causes us to smile and laugh at army scenes. It is too serious a matter. Those of my age that look back know the troubles through which we have passed.

We can say to you younger people something of the cost of this nation.

I don't know how many there are on the pension list, but I am not on it for the war of the rebellion. I kept off of it for this reason: I am not yet willing, as a general officer, to receive a pension as long as there is a private soldier that is deprived of his pension. (Applause.) No application of mine is on file at the Department of Washington. I have been asked, too, to allow the Congressmen, in this wonderful state of Iowa, to let them introduce a bill to grant me a magnificent pension. No, ladies and gentlemen, I could not accept it as long as the private soldier is deprived of his pension. Patriotism is what is needed in this country. You people of the normal school, you younger ladies of the country, take for example the defense of this nation by the old soldiers, and particularly those that defended it at the Hornets' Nest of Shiloh. A gentleman intimated to me this morning that some one was intimating to him, that we who held there so long were taking too much credit to ourselves. Great heavens! Why didn't you look after our reputations whilst we were down south suffering, and you up here living off the fat of the land? Patriotism of the right kind is needed in this country. What is that? An educated patriotism. That is what it is. No man in this country has a right, under the laws of our land, to be a brute in feeling. No man has the privilege under the guise of liberty in this country to make a home unhappy. Too many unhappy wives and children in this country today. Educate to a higher plane. What will do it? I will tell you. Look at that flag, every one of you; plant it in every school room of America. Keep it there. Explain to the rising generation what it means. Not only the emblem of liberty, but the emblem of a nation's pride. It was that flag that you men suffered in upholding. Teach it to the children of this country that the soldier that raised his hands and eyes to Almighty God, took the oath of allegiance beneath that flag, swore to defend it, protect it and serve his country beneath its folds; let the children understand that that obligation meant something more than mere battle. It meant to lead the armies on, to educate the public of this land. Normal students, listen. In twenty years from today it will be impossible, unless we educate differently, to make the young man of the country and the young lady of the country understand that this great nation of ours, this proud and mighty country of ours, ever endorsed that deadly institution of slavery as it existed at one time. It will be impossible to make them believe that the American people ever placed upon the auction block the mother, stripping the infant from the breast, and selling that mother as a chattel. Educate. We are making great progress; think of it, you normal students. In 1849 it took some of your fathers and friends four months to cross the mighty plain, seeking a few dollars in the hills of California. Today you can start at Boston Monday morning Friday afternoon you take supper in the beautiful city of San Francisco, California. What did it? You boys that took the oath of allegiance beneath that flag. You boys that carried it successfully and won the victory and sustained the union of states. Since that day, all over this mighty country, you can travel by steam, by rail. Think of it. What caused it? Sustaining the union of States. Yes, says some. Now don't be alarmed. I have got too much sense to switch off on to a side track here. Someone says, oh, it costs so much money. We have got to have more. Go to work and earn more, everyone of you in this country. That is what is wanted. (Applause.) I never heard of two soldiers complaining of this government. Why, God bless you normal students, we have got the best government on the face of the earth. Surpassing all nations in everything that pertains to greatness. We have the greater men; we have the better soil; we have the greatest extent of country, more lines of railroad, more telegraph communication, more telephones, longer and better and handsomer rivers than any nation on earth, and decidedly better looking ladies than any on the face of God Almighty's earth. What is it made them happy? Not money. Not money. I don't know, my dear brother, but what there is too much money in the country. I can get along with a nickle. I have only ten cents today that I can call my own. Poverty. I have suffered the stings of poverty in this nation that I claim to have done some little to defend, and yet there is not wealth enough in the nation to make me repudiate one single dollar of national indebtedness. Patriotism is what is needed in this country and none better, gentlemen of the Iowa Hornets' Nest Brigade, none better to keep it in the state of Iowa than you. Every true soldier understands that. Great God, what a country we have, but, oh, sometimes how it is managed. (Applause) I could run this country I think I could run it if I had the privilege. I once thought I had got the privilege but they sent me to prison and I couldn't get out in time. (Applause.)

Yesterday a gentleman handed me this program. I noticed that Capt. McCormick was not to be here and your president asked me if I would respond for him. His subject was "After Shiloh, prison." Capt. McCormick was to respond. I consented to respond but afterwards we made a change. I wanted to go home. Had I responded to that I would have had to tell you army stories. I was thinking of it, but when reflecting, gentlemen, something else must be said and done at reunions besides telling army stories, besides misrepresenting certain scenes, I thought I had better not embark in that direction and thus I stayed over a day to talk to you soldiers today.

Gentlemen of this Hornets' Nest Brigade of Iowa, I like every one of you. I doubly respect and like those that were captured with me there at Shiloh. I know what you passed through in those prisons; I know what your fare was; I know how your Colonel suffered; I know what they lived on; the kind of soup they had. I know full well that I sold a nice gold watch to get Confederate scrip to keep an Iowa soldier alive, and that colonel was the colonel of the 8th Iowa—J. L. Geddes. God bless him. He suffered; scores suffered. Ferguson died in prison. Oh, the sights that we behold when we reflect. Today for the first time I learned that you had a Tennesseean in the 8th Iowa, three of them. One was captured and shot, by the name of Roland. The other is a nice gentleman living in Tennessee today. I was telling him that we met from three to four hundred of those poor east Tennesseeans in a starving condition. We divided our rations with them. I am telling this that you young people may know what these people passed through. You officers remember there when we tore up the floor and we received our first rations, we divided it with the hungry Tennesseeans by dropping it through the hole in the floor. How they grabbed for that provision. They were American citizens. They had been misled, some of them of the south, as they acknowledge today and I hate and despise those who misled them. Let me tell you, it is the arrant demagogue of our country who causes all the trouble. There were not to exceed 150 men that were responsible for that great rebellion. They were led astray. Appeals were made to them. Oh, how pleasant, then, they receive this information today. Tell it to them. They will listen and realize the truth as it is told, and they profit by it, too. I may say this. Down there upon that bloody field of Shiloh, in that county, from the day of the battle up to the present time, it has been a loyal county to the union of the United States of America, and is today. I would that every county in the state was in the same condition. But how can we get them there? Educate. That is what it is. Go with me down into my state. Ryan, I told a soldier today I lived in Missouri. Says he, the devil you do. Says he, what are you living there for? Why, people of Iowa, let me tell you. We have a grand population in the state of Missouri. We have one of the grandest states of the union, made so by the war; that is what made it. We got rid of that pecular institution whose darkness seemed to prevail in certain districts of the state, even to this late day, thirty years after it has been swept from American soil. We suffer from it yet but we are rid of the institution by law and we are coming to the front. Mark what I tell you. Seventy-six years of age but there are listening to me today a hundred people that will live to see the state of Missouri the second state of the Union in population, wealth and grandeur. It is coming. We have a grand country. Why, people of Iowa, we are decent people down there. We go to church down in Missouri. We have abundance of ministers. We don't pay them quite enough, and you normal students, let me tell you, don't come to Missouri expecting to teach school. Why God bless you, we are grinding out school teachers there, a hundred to where there is one can get employment. Abundance of them. We are educating in that wonderful state. When I went to the state of Missouri I couldn't have taken that beautiful banner in my hand and talked plainly without being insulted. Today I can go into any township of the state of Missouri; I can defend that flag, I can say what I please in its defense; I can portray the horrors of the old institution; I can persuade those people how they were misled in the rebellion. They listen and as I raise the flag and ask them to renew allegiance to it, not a soul will refuse, not one. Why, what has become of them. I will tell you what has become of them. Those that don't like the flag, they don't go to meeting. That is, to my kind of meeting. So help me God, ladies, if I was a minister of the gospel, no sermon would ever be preached by me unless the stars and stripes were in my pulpit. (Loud applause)

Now, friends, it is patriotism we want in this country. It is not republicans. It is not democrats. It is not that other set. (Laughter) It is not them we want. You people of Iowa found that out. But I will tell you what we want. We want christian people true to the flag, true to the country, true to the union schools of the country, true to the churches, true to humanity, true to their families. Confound the lazy, trifling cuss that will marry a decent woman and have a family and fail to support them well, he ought to join the other—— (Laughter.)

Ladies and gentlemen, now, you see, I claim to be a patriot, and I claim for the Iowa brigade that every mother's son of them is a true patriot, and if any of them dodge, just put them beneath the flag and administer the oath anew again. Thus let me appeal to the young. Take the advice of an old man, 76 years of age, talking to you here today and appealing for his country. I know the danger that threatens this land today. It is a dangerous element that comes to this country, not knowing what liberty means in this land. That is what it is. He that is a true American likes every American institution in this country and he likes to protect them, too. Now don't take that in a political sense, but it will apply awfully well if you did. (Applause) Why, young man, I am a true American. I like everything that is made in America. All you fellows like bicycles, don't you? If you don't you are different from us Missouri lads; and, ladies, let me say to you, I have made up my mind, the first extra 10, 20 or 30 dollars I get, to buy a second-hand bicycle and commence riding. (Laughter) I want to encourage American institutions. I want to keep the money at home and make a market for every American that is willing to toil for a dollar, and confound the fellow that wants somebody to give him a dollar.

Ladies and gentlemen, patriotism is what we need. Is a man a patriot that will go to Ohio, to New England, and borrow a thousand dollars, come home, mortgage his home to pay it, when he fails to pay the interest and principal, goes to damning them for loaning him a thousand dollars? What do you think of such a fellow? Ladies, never marry one of the young men of that kind. Let them alone. Those fellows will work out their own salvation after they have starved a year or two. True Americanism is what we want; true patriotism is what we need in this country. Let us sustain every institution that defends right and justice. As I am to talk in the square, let me appeal to you old soldiers, if you don't like the laws of this country, obey them anyhow. (Cries, "That is right!") Obey every law. Don't violate the laws of our country. Don't violate the laws of God. Do right. Administer justice everywhere. If you have got an old justice of the peace that hasn't sense enough to administer the laws of this country, or a constable or a sheriff, and I know you haven't here in Jasper county, but if you have, the sooner you get them out of possession the better for the rising generation.

Ladies and gentlemen, I am pleased to have met you here this afternoon. I know it is warm. I have an esteemed comrade here. I am not going to let Ryan introduce him. He has been a general — in the army. He was in the eastern army. He is a better looking gentleman, if possible, than the one now talking to you; and that is an acknowledgment that I don't often make. But I have known my friend so long. He is a good natured gentleman. I believe he will endorse every utterance I have made, with the exception of the little rough language that I have put in here and there, but I will seek forgiveness for that. You know I am a pretty good Methodist and they, when they get a little off of their base and get a little excited, sometimes say things that had better not be said. If I have said it today, and it wounds the feeling of anyone here or sounds harsh, forgive me. I have a right to talk plain.. Let me ask again of you young people of the country, get you a flag, look at it, and see if it doesn't come up — I don't know that I can quote the stanza a little boy of mine composed and said, that is pretty good, get that off over in Iowa. I got it off in one or two places of the state, too. It is this:

"Take the flag; put it in your pulpit; put it in the school house, and learn your children to exclaim, as I do mine:
Now, great emblem of the brave,
With purpose fixed we stand;
Ready to battle, ready to save
The pride and honor of this land.
Wave o'er the country from on high.
Wave o'er the halt and lame.
Wave on! We will battle till we die
To save that honor—fame."

God bless the flag of our country! Don't you say so, too? Now, with me, as one of the defenders of the flag, I have one request to make. I want every one in this audience, in the presence of General B. M. Prentiss, that loves that flag, I want him to hurrah. Old and young, arise to your feet. Now with me, renewing our allegiance to the flag of our country, give three cheers to the flag as I cheer. Wait—and you ladies get your handkerchiefs in your hands—you needn't cheer, but just wave your handkerchiefs as the men cheer. Boys and gentlemen, all together—three cheers for the flag of our nation and its laws! (Hip, hip, hurrah! hurrah! hurrah!)

Now, ladies and gentlemen, having that pledge from you, I can go to Missouri a happy man.

Col. Ryan then introduced Gen. Osborn, of Chicago, in the following words:

"I now have the extreme pleasure of introducing one of my old friends from Illinois, General Osborn, who was appointed by General Grant minister to Buenos Ayres; the handsome and accomplished gentleman who was minister there for sixteen years in succession. General Osborn, my friends. Come forward, my General. I have talked him to sleep nearly. Ladies and gentlemen, General Osborn, of Chicago."

GENERAL OSBORN.

Ladies and Gentlemen:

Since coming here I, too, have caught the spirit, and I would gladly talk to you, but Judge Ryan wont let me. So I bid you good-afternoon.

JUDGE RYAN.

"*Ladies and Gentlemen:*

"That is a——— Next on the program is music."

After music, the meeting adjourned to the court yard, where General Prentiss spoke to an immense crowd.

After that, preparations were begun for the parade, and in a short time it was formed, and an imposing procession it made. The order was as follows:

Marshals—M. A. McCord and O. C. Meredith.
K. T. Band, led by Drum Major on horseback.
Co. L, I. N. G.
Newton Fire Department.
Normal Institute Students, three hundred strong, headed by Miss Walsh in a carriage.
Garrett Post, G. A. R.
W. R. C.
L. of G. A. R.
Martial Band of nine pieces.
Hornets' Nest Brigade.

The line of march was taken just as advertised and terminated at the east side of the school house, where seats had been built to accommodate the crowd. The exercises were under the direction of Normal school. After a spirited duet given by two little daughters of S. E. Laird, Prof. D. M. Kelly extended the following welcome to the Brigade in behalf of the Normal. The address was permeated with a spirit of the truest patriotism and noblest manhood:

Ladies and Gentlemen:

As a young man I feel most highly honored by the invitation extended to me to appear on this occasion as a representative of that loyal brigade of Jasper county teachers, voicing as best I may the respect, veneration and love they bear for that immortal brigade of grizzled veterans who honor us and the cause we represent by the very fact of their presence.

We can say to you nothing that is new. We can add no new honors to these soldiers living or to their comrades dead. We can surround with no new glory a subject that is already glorified in every loyal heart that throbs and beats beneath the Stars and Stripes. We can offer you, our honored guests, only the tribute of praise and gratitude that is due from our generation to your generation. We can offer you only the tribute of praise that is due from the protected to the protectors living and the protectors dead.

What we have gleaned from the pages of history, you men who honor us with your presence, gleaned from the pages of bitter experience. What we have heard of the ravages and the spirit of war, you saw and with your own eyes. You were the actors in that great and awful tragedy of civil strife. We are but the camp followers reaping the rewards of your exertions.

I am afraid that we sometimes forget what courage, devotion and patriotism were displayed by our soldiers in the late war. Some of them returned and they are with us yet. Some returned but their stay was only brief. Some died upon the field of battle and ashes mingle with ashes in the long and ghastly trench. Some died in prison, cruel, cruel death! and their forms are now mouldering in the bosom of their mother Earth. Some died from pestilence and exposure and are now resting peacefully in graves unknown and uncared for.

It must be hard to die, even at home in the arms of father or mother, but what must it be to die far from home and mother, without a friend to lift the sinking head; without a hand to wipe the death dew from the failing eyes; torn by bullets and sabers; crushed by flying splinters and the trampling hoof. Homeless, friendless, nameless, dying. No one to see, no eye to pity, but the eye of the Great God of battles.

Oh, it is hard to die! The green fields, the singing birds, the happy homes are hard to yield for that narrow house and the crawling worm. The bright flowers nod their heads to us and bid us stay. The blue sky spreads wide her arms and entreats us not to die. There is something in the heart of every sane man that tells him he must live. "Self preservation is the first law of human nature," yet these soldiers did not falter in the time of danger. The father kissed his baby and then was ready for the sacrifice. The son received his mother's blessing and went out to battle for his country, for his home, for liberty and for us, and are we truly grateful? Do we realize the good they gave us? Would you cross the ocean into England, France, Germany—the Stars and Stripes are at once your passport and safeguard. In the fastnesses of the Himalayas or in the jungles of the Amazon, wrapped in the flag of the United States, you are safe in time of danger. At home or abroad, in peace or in war, that flag is ever your faithful guardian and friend.

It has been steeped in loyal blood; it has been powder stained and bullet torn; it has been furled in honorable defeat and reared aloft in many a hard won victory; it has waved over the heights of Lookout Mountain and sunk beneath the dark waters of the Mississippi; but thank God no stain now mars its striped field, no jewel is missing from its starry crown. On Shi'oh's battle ground, an emblem of justice, it lay folded close in the heart of every loyal son of Iowa, tied round with the tenderest cords of his affection and sealed with a vow never to surrender it up until that heart was cold and still in death.

Upon every school-house in the state of Iowa, that banner should float, float, an emblem of patriotism, of liberty and of unsullied honor.

In the great ledger of Justice from 1860 to 1865, liberty is credited by names and deeds that years of infamy will not over balance.

Turn to that page, 'tis open to all—heading these lists of credits will be found the name of Lincoln; following close after comes the name of your beloved commander Grant. Memories cluster round those names, "Memories of the days that tried the souls of men." Here is a cluster of names blotted and tear stained and we know that Shiloh's dead are entered here; upon this crimson page the heroes of Gettysburg; upon that the slain on the fatal field by Fredericksburg. Oh, my soldier friends, praise is all that I can give you. I never heard the whistle of an enemy's bullet, you heard many. I never ministered to the wants of a friend, cut down in defense of the old flag. You ministered to the wants of a brother, you moistened his lips from your old canteen and you buried him far from home and friends, all because he loved that old flag. I never saw a comrade starving, rotting, dying in a prison pen because he refused to take the oath of allegiance to a state in rebellion. You did. You tried it yourselves, many of you to the extreme limit of endurance, your bowed forms and shrunken limbs still testify thereto. I never even did battle for my country or my home. You did both, upon the hillside, in the valley and by the stream. Your bunk mate lies buried by the Father of Waters, your comrades in the swamps of Alabama and the cotton fields of Georgia. Where e're they rest 'tis hallowed ground, watered by their blood and a nation's tears. Teachers, never before have we been so honored. We have now before us the grandest object lesson of patriotism that our time shall ever know. Let the lesson sink deep into your hearts and establish there a renewed determination to teach well the great lesson of *love for America and for American institutions.*

Here in the shadow of this sanctuary, the grandest in America, made possible by the patriotism and devotion of these men and such as these; here in the shadow of the free school, the birth-place of American liberty; here in the shadow of this school house, from which floats, thanks to these men and such as these, that beautiful emblem of red, white and blue; here in the presence of these teachers, whose sentiments I am called on to express, in their names and in the names of the school children of Iowa, I place my hand upon the walls of this building, the free school of America, and proclaim honor to you as friends, love to you as soldiers, and veneration to you as patriotic defenders of liberty and union!

Prof. Kelly's address of welcome was responded to by L. Kinkead, 8th Iowa, and R. M. Terrill, of the 12th Iowa. We regret that we cannot present them as both were good, but all our efforts to get their manuscripts have failed. They will be court martialed at our next reunion, for disobedience of orders.

The Brigade at the close of the exercises marched to headquarters and disbanded.

Camp Fire.

❦ ❦ ❦

The Brigade assembled at head quarters at 7:30 p. m. and escorted by the drum corps, marched to the opera house. Col. Ryan presided at the Camp Fire.

The exercises were opened by an earnest prayer by Rev. Harrah, followed by a solo, "Tenting on the Old Camp Ground," by Fred Hough. The first speaker introduced was Col. Godfrey, of the 2d Iowa, "Johnson's Surrender to Sherman." The main points are only given in the paper at the request of the Col.:

"JOHNSON'S SURRENDER TO SHERMAN" BY COL. G. L. GODFREY."

Ladies and Gentlemen, and Comrades:

I appear before you to night under rather embarrassing circumstances, not so much so now, not so embarrassing since I have been here and met your people and received the cordial hospitality that I have, as I was when I started from home. A little embarrassing because Mr. Ryan presided here tonight. There may be difficulty between Ryan and me, he being the chairman he has got the advantage of me, but I want to say to the members of the Hornets' Nest Brigade, that you will never appreciate, you will never fully know and cannot appreciate because you do not know the work that this chairman has done to forward the interest of getting up this reunion. Now if he has written you half as many letters as he has me in regard to it, he must have employed all the typewriters in Newton, and I do not know but that is the case. Why it got so in the morning mail, if the children in bringing in the mail didn't see a letter with Dave Ryan's name in the upper corner of it, they would say, "What do you suppose is the matter with Mr. Ryan? Is he sick?" That is the fact. He was in great distress about getting somebody to talk for the 2d Iowa. I proposed this man, and that man, and other men, and he couldn't get fixed, and finally I told him I had a paper that I had prepared to read before another military organization, that would take from ten to fifteen minutes, and that as a last resort I could bring that paper down. Well, now the cordial reply I got to that was, "Well, Colonel, bring down the paper and if we can't do any better we will let you read it." Well, that was pretty good. I felt pretty good over that. That was only equalled, though, by the earnest solicitation I had from another member from Newton about my coming here, and that is a member also that I have seen working in the interests of this organization since I have been here—I refer to Col. Manning. Now Mr. Ryan came up to Des Moines and came before the committee and asked the committee to bring the organization here this time. He says, "The people of Newton will entertain the Hornets' Nest Brigade, free." Oh, says I, "That won't do; what authority have you got for saying that?" He says, "I have got the authority of the mayor and everybody in Newton." "What will you do with us? You haven't got a hotel large enough." "Well, we will parcel you out among the people." Well the committee decided to come here. A few weeks after that, Col. Manning came to Des Moines—it was during the state convention—he came into a room in the Savery House, where I was sitting. Now you know the Colonel has got one of the most beaming faces in the world; he is a handsome man also, but he has got a pocket in that face where he keeps his stock all stored and disguised, and he can open that pocket and spread it all over his face better than any other man that I ever saw. He came in and he had his face disguised, when he saw me sitting there. Says I, "Good morning." "Good morning." "When did you come up?" "Just got in," said he; "We had a meeting down to Newton this morning." "A meeting?" "Yes." "Well, what about?" "Oh, about your confounded Brigade." "Well, what of it?" He says, "It falls to my lot to have to entertain you while down there." Well that was encouraging, but I told him if I could stand it two days, I thought he could. Well, I have been here and I have been to his house two days and he is still alive and so am I, thanks to his good wife. And I feel as though I wanted the largest hearted man here to offer some resolutions of thanks. I believe there is a committee appointed, though. Well, I hope the committee will cover all these things in their thanks, and there is one thing further that I hope they will not forget that struck me, and that is this. The recitation we had last night, on "Shiloh Battlefield at Night." I had never heard it before. I hope there did not any of you see me sitting back here in the corner wiping my eyes at the recitation of that. If you did, I hope you will not call me a baby. But it was grand. Now the mayor told in his opening speech, "Boys, if you see anything that you want, take it. If you can't reach it, ask any of the citizens of Newton to hand it down to you." Now I want to ask some of the citizens of Newton to hand down that beautiful young lady that recited that piece to us last night that we may shake hands with her and thank her for the entertainment that she gave us. [Applause.]

But now to this paper. I am not going to read it all.

The Col. then read a paper on the surrender of Johnson to Gen. Sherman. The paper sustained Gen. Sherman in his first agreement with Johnson, which agreement was disapproved by President Johnson, (President Lincoln having been killed a few days previous to Johnson's surrender.) That Sherman had consulted with Lincoln just a few days before, at City Point, the paper took the grounds that Sherman was carrying out the policy of President Lincoln and sustained this view by liberal quotations from the conversations between Lincoln, Grant and Admiral Porter, had at City Point, just a few days previous to the surrender, and in closing the paper censured severely the newspapers which published the unfriendly criticisms against Sherman, and also Secretary of War Stanton and Gen. Halleck for their ill conduct toward Gen. Sherman, as brave and patriotic a commander as ever led an army.

Prof. A. N. Currier gave us the following excellent paper, which gave evidence of much thought in its preparation:

"THE LONG ROLL."

Ladies and Gentlemen:

I am really afraid that some of these younger people will remember the old soldier who fought a little a good many years ago, and ever since that time have talked about it when they got a chance, but you have made a very grave mistake if you make so severe a judgment against us. This is only one of our spells, but as the Hornets' Nest Brigade have only one of these spells, once in three years, I think you may put up with it, but still I am afraid that after these speeches are over, you may think a new definition of speeches which I have heard will be very appropriate. It is a definition that is not found in Webster or the Standard dictionary, or the Encyclopedia or the Century, but is taken from the bicycle. Somebody has said, that a great many speeches are pneumatic tires. I will say to you that my "tire" shall be very short, because I heard what Col. Ryan said, and having risked my life a few times thirty years ago I do not propose to endanger it tonight. When this speech was assigned me—for I did not choose it myself—I only accepted it because, as a soldier, I had learned that when Col. Bell gave the command I must obey. It would seem a grievous sin against the proprieties to make the beating of the Long Roll the prelude to a speech. In war times, certainly, it was never a call to words, but a cry to arms, to arms! that put the blood astir in our veins and sent it tingling to our finger tips. After these thirty years of peace, it calls up anew and most vividly many a stirring scene and hard fought struggle, but at this moment, most of all, the bloody field of Shiloh—to most of us the first experience of a real battlefield. The Long Roll on that memorable morning came to us as an utter surprise. There had, indeed, been some stray shots on the picket line during the night, and we heard the firing at the front that took place when the outmost regiments were surprised while yet asleep in their camps. But there was no thought of a general engagement in which we should share. The routine of Sunday morning went on quite undisturbed. Divine services were announced for 11 o'clock and inspection was going on on the color line of the 8th when the order came from Brigade headquarters, directing the beating of the Long Roll and preparations for an immediate march to the battlefield. There was a quiver in Adjt. Sam Rankin's voice as he reported the order and Cooney's nervous fingers for a moment forgot their cunning but it was only for a moment and then the Roll was beaten in dead earnest that said, "to arms, to arms!" with more emphasis than any words could do. They thrilled us like an electric shock and it seemed as if their echo reached regiment after regiment and brigade after brigade as the call sounded again and again and the excitement and bustle surged through all that great camp, which up to that moment had seemed more like a great picnic than a theatre of war. Everybody was greatly excited, but if there was fear in their heart there was none in the faces or the actions of our men. Those who had been ill and off duty, claimed to be well again, and those on special duty asked to be released from their details. One thing alone weighed upon our spirits, Col. Geddes was under arrest and we might be compelled to go into battle without him. We all felt that it would be a great misfortune to be deprived of his experience, his skill and his bravery at such a crisis. But, however, he is released from arrest and amid the shouts of the men leads us to the field. I shall not attempt to describe the events of that bloody field. Marked as it was by serious disaster, it was still more marked by the high courage and stubborn resistance against superior force. Those of us who fell into the hands of the enemy on Sunday evening had not then, and have not now, any apology to offer for that misfortune. We could not be driven from our post by the repeated and violent attacks of the enemy. We inflicted losses out of all proportion to those we suffered. Those who did not die in their tracks were overwhelmed and captured with their faces to the foe. It was our misfortune and not our fault that we did not share in the dearly bought victory of Monday. Serious as were the Union losses from the lack of foresight and preparation on the part of Grant and Sherman, as well as from the courage and skill of the enemy, Shiloh was a victory of great consequence to our cause. Grant's pluck and capacity in action were displayed in a greater battle than heretofore, but more than all else, the metal of the western armies was tested in a supreme effort and found to be of the finest and best. The bluster and swagger in rebel quarters stopped short, there was no more talk of one rebel being as good as three Yankees, and both armies realized, as never before, the seriousness and magnitude of the conflict.

Comrades, it is hard to believe that a third of a century lies between us and those events, so fresh in our memory and thoughts, and yet it is not hard to realize it when we look into each others faces and behold the traces of the years in features and forms. Then we were boys, or young men, full of life and energy, now our hair is gray, or white, and our step is less elastic—men call us old, but I assert that we are yet young and vigorous and fit for service, whenever and wherever the drum beat of duty summons us to arms. The country is indeed saved and safe from rebels, and is Union in a truer and fuller sense than ever before, but our term of service is not over, if we are the true men we claim to be. What was worth saving at such a cost of blood and treasure, must be kept as a sacred trust and handed over to the generations to come, without spot or blemish. Not on the far off fields of the south, but in our very midst, must the battle be fought against the violators of the sanctity of the law through chicane, or corruptions, or open violence, against the enemies of our public schools, the enemies of a pure and free ballot, against the foes of the perfect freedom of labor and of the equality of all American citizens in rights and privileges without regard to color, ancestry or religious creed.

Comrades of the Grand Army of the Republic, we have shown how a million citizens, attached to their homes and devoted to the pursuits of peace, could be transformed, for love of country, into valiant soldiers. We have shown how a mighty army, flushed with victory, could gladly lay down its arms and resume the duties and occupations of civil life. Let us continue to show how gray haired veterans ever true to Old Glory—our free and stainless flag, can do conspicuous service to the land we fought to save, with no furlough and no discharge until the final muster out.

Miss Belle Lambert gave an excellent rendering of "Money Musk" of which the audience showed their appreciation by their loud applause.

Then came singing, after which H. G. Curtis, of the 8th Iowa, was drafted to fill the place of one of the speakers who was absent and who was to have talked about "The man that carried a gun," and responded in a brief and telling manner as follows:

Comrades:

I came here to listen, not to talk. I am not on the program but I am one of those boys that carried a gun. I am one of the fellows that helped put down this rebellion, and I belonged to a regiment that helped to do it, and to a Brigade that helped to do it. Now you say, how was this done anyhow? The boys loved their country; the girls loved the boys; a combination that was invincible. (Loud applause.)

Wm. T. McMakin, of the 14th Iowa, as the last speaker, had the subject, "We took touch of elbows." As he stated, the paper was confined principally to the 14th Iowa, but it was no doubt a like experience of many of the other comrades.

Mr. Chairman, Ladies and Gentlemen, and Comrades:

Comrades: I want to take you back, let your minds revert back some thirty years ago. Do you recollect when you were recruits? I am a raw recruit tonight and yet I feel that I can stand as a soldier if I can do nothing else, if I cannot say a word tonight I can point to that old flag that contains the history of all of us. I feel, comrades, tonight, that it is good to be here. I feel that we have in these associations and these reunions, that we again take the "touch of elbow." We feel the grasp of the hand; we fight over our battles again; we renew our age; we live longer for enjoying these things. I know many of our comrades and I would refer you to our old commander of the 14th Iowa—look at the difference as he appears upon the stage, as he appeared before you and addressed you. He is old in years yet how supple he is; young in heart as any of us.

What I shall say tonight will be principally in relation to the 14th Iowa, as my history is in that as a private, and I feel that tie existing as you all feel, and comrades, while there is a tie existing running between all of this great army, yet there is a tie of regiment, yet there is an inner tie of company. I would draw the attention of the comrades to a question that has never been brought up as I see, that the 14th Iowa was the largest regiment that went from the state of Iowa, not in number of members but in companies. We had first, three; we had again, seven, then three more, making in all thirteen companies that were organized and in the 14th Iowa, not at one time, however. And I would again call the attention of the 14th Iowa that our extent of service was as great as any regiment that ever went from the state of Iowa. Now the first active campaign that I experienced was at Ft. Henry. You recollect that we were booked for that place but we got in a little too late to capture the Fort. It was taken. We landed upon the bank near Ft. Henry. You recollect we lay there over the Sabbath day. Well on Sabbath morning while we were some of us writing and some of us doing various work, down through that camp charged a beef animal. Well, we wanted fresh meat. We grasped our gun, I with the rest, not knowing who was with me, and after that animal we started. Down we went and I fired at it, and a man at my right hand fired; at that I looked around to see who it was and it was our chaplain. Well, I thought I was in good company if I had the chaplain, but the worst of that thing, comrades, was, they sent word right back home that McMakin and the chaplain were out stealing cattle. Now that wasn't so; we wasn't stealing; there was no stealing in the army, it was either capturing or confiscating. You remember, comrades, when we were taken prisoners at Shiloh. I pass over that; there has been enough said on that today and I cannot do any better, no, not half as well as those who have spoken before me. But you remember when we were captured and taken to Memphis, that we were quartered in that old commission house on the banks of the Mississippi. You recollect how crowded our quarters were at that time; we hadn't room to lie down, part of us had to stand up. After we had been there two or three days the commissioned officers came to the door and said if there was any communication that we wished to send back to our friends in the north that he would see that it was carried with a flag of truce which they expected in a few days, in fact they looked for the capture of Memphis. If we would write an open letter, he would see that it was taken.

So my comrades wrote a letter to the Burlington Hawkeye, giving the names of that company and our condition there. That we were all well, none of us wounded, and that we were having enough to eat for the present. We wanted to alleviate the fears of those friends that were north, that had heard nothing, as many of the comrades can testify here tonight. We knew the anxiety there was at home, and how much anxiety there was in those days to hear from those boys. We gave the letter into the hands of the officer. He went out with it. On the night following I was standing at the door of the entrance that went out into the hall and one of the private guards that stood there—you know, comrades, that those guards were principally Union men at heart—told me that night privately, says he, that letter will never go. If you will write a letter, I am going to leave this place if the Union troops don't capture it in a few days, I will see that your letter goes to your lines. I took from my pocket a leaf, I had an envelope, and I wrote a letter to my wife in Des Moines county, and gave it to him and addressed it. That was the only letter, the only word, with the exception of one that I heard came to a member of the 8th Iowa, from the same person or mailed at the same place. I don't know whether that is true, perhaps I may get a response to it, but that letter was mailed in another envelope, in Illinois, and came safely to my wife, the first and only word that came from our boys.

Now, comrades, I must say a word of tribute to our old commander. We have had many commanders of troops in this state, many colonels, but, comrades of the Fourteenth, where is the man, where is the officer that went from Iowa that you would exchange for our old colonel, William T. Shaw, of Anamosa?

This was followed by a solo, "The Vacant Chair," beautifully rendered by Mr. H. M. Vaughan.

The Committee on Resolutions then presented the following report, which was adopted:

Resolved, That it is the sense of the Hornets' Nest Brigade that the legislature of Iowa should, at its coming session, appropriate a sufficient sum of money for the erection of a monument befitting the wealth and dignity of our state, on the battlefield of Shiloh, to commemorate the valor of the Iowa soldiers on that bloody field.

Resolved, That a committee consisting of one from each regiment of this brigade, be appointed, whose duty it shall be, in conjunction with other Iowa regiments, to impress upon the next general assembly the duty of making an appropriation of from $75,000 to $100,000 for the purpose of carrying into execution the object herein set forth.

Resolved, That this association returns its sincere thanks to the patriotic citizens of Newton and vicinity for the great interest they have taken in the success of this meeting, as well as in the comfort and happiness of everyone in attendance; for the free use of this opera house and other rooms, and for the music and literary features of the several programs. We have been made to feel at home by a most cordial welcome, and by every kindness and courtesy that a generous people could extend, for all of which the town of Newton will always be gratefully remembered and esteemed by this association.

S. A. MOORE,
J. W. AKERS,
W. B. BELL,   Committee.
T. B. EDGINGTON,
S. CHAPMAN,

Col. Bell of the 8th Iowa then insisted that Col. Ryan, though modest, should favor us with a speech and said, "It was made the duty of the senior officers of the several regiments to name parties who were to appear and take part in this camp fire. I am sorry to say that one of those it was my duty to name did not appear, and it is the first time in all my recollection that ever he failed to obey my command, and that is our chairman. I do not know whether it was because of modesty because he is at home, but now I insist on it that we hear from our worthy chairman, Col. Ryan."

Col. Ryan overcame his modesty and replied:

Ladies and Gentlemen:

It affords me very great pleasure that I have an opportunity to stand before you tonight for I have something special that I desire to say. I want to say first, that I feel glad that we were permitted to meet the comrades of the Hornets' Nest Brigade here in the city of Newton. But there is something else that I desire to say. Comrade Burns and myself are the only two comrades that belong to this Brigade that reside in the city of Newton. When we came home and reported what we had done, and that the Brigade desired to spend their next reunion with us, we went first to the Post, the Grand Army Post, No. 16, Grand Army of the Republic. Immediately they said thus, "Whatever you desire, name it and you shall have it." We were not modest in our request and we asked that there be various committees appointed and there has not been a single person appointed upon any one of those committees but has responded most heartily. Our town has been canvassed, notwithstanding the fact that there were over 300 teachers attending normal school here. Now we were not aware of that at the time the date was fixed, and I confess it was with a great deal of timidity when I learned that fact that we sent out this committee and asked them what doors would open. I want to say, my fellow citizens, that I thank you from the very bottom of my heart. It touched my feelings when the committee came in and said there was not a single door in all the town but swung open upon its hinges to receive my comrades of the Hornets' Nest Brigade. [Applause] There has not been a single request that has been made but what has been responded to. We went to our city fathers and they said to us, "Gentlemen, name what you wish." The mayor has expressed and it was no buncombe, it was no simple words for sound only, it stated to you the naked facts, that the gates of the city were thrown open.

There was nothing that we have demanded and I want to say that it was an easy matter, it made it a matter so easy that it has been a pleasure to assist in the organization of this reunion that we have had here. Now I want to say further that I made it my business to inquire of the comrades; I hadn't much else to do. The committees took everything else off of my hands at my request and at the request of comrade Burns, and have executed everything that we requested, and so I say I had little to do but sit around and ask the comrades how they were received and what sort of quarters they had in general ways and special ways, and everyone of them have said: "Such magnificent treatment we have never received before." That made my heart glad too, fellow citizens. For them I want to stand before you tonight and in the presence of the company that yet remain, to thank you for the generous entertainment that you have extended to them. And more let me say, that it puts me under such obligation that any time I can be of service to you under like or similar circumstances, my doors and my home are open to you. I do not desire to take your time in talking. Here at the end of this program I know that you don't desire to be entertained, but this much I do want to say of the magnificent music that we have had. All that I had to do was to make a single suggestion, and it is fair that we say, that so many offers were made of hospitality, that though we feared that we would not be able to accommodate all that came, there were a hundred and more places for other comrades had they come. The next time when you come to Newton, do not come with your brigade alone, come with your division, come in solid phalanx, come one, come all, and the doors of Newton, the gates of the city will be open, a welcome will be extended to you, our hands will be outstretched to you. Comrades, God bless you. I know we will not all meet again. God bless you.

Much feeling was expressed at the close of the camp fire.

In closing we feel it would be proper to make mention of some of those who so materially aided in making our Reunion such a grand success, and for the kindness and hospitality shown us: to Col. D. Ryan who is entitled to great credit for his zeal and untiring efforts, always in the thick of the fight; Mrs Rodgers and Miss Townsend, who had charge of the singing, and to all the singers who so ably seconded their efforts; nor would we forget the little ones who at the opening exercises sang so beautifully; Col. Manning, who acted as quartermaster and commissary, and his assistants, Mrs. S. S Patterson and Mrs. O. C. Meredith the Col. would make a good Hornet, we'll take him in; Rob't. Burns, he is already a Hornet and is all O. K.; Miss Beamen, the stenographer, who by her skill has enabled us to give you the extempore speeches; the G. A. R., we've touched elbows; and finally to one and all of the citizens of Newton, thanks for your kindness and hospitality, ever remembered and never forgotten.

Hornets' Nest Roster.

The following is a list of the members of the Brigade who were present and registered:

2nd IOWA INFANTRY.

COMPANY B.

Mennig, Geo., Sheldon, Iowa
Dow, Albert, Newton, Iowa
Worth, L. A., Southerland, Ia.
Park, J. C., West Liberty
Heilman, J. S., Bennett, Iowa
Smallenburg, M., Buffalo, N. Y., [806 Eagle St.]
Quinn, A. J., New Sharon, Iowa
Thompson, M. L., Earlham, Iowa

COMPANY C.

Albright, Chas. F., Primghar, Ia.
McNeil, H. C., Sioux City, Iowa
Rodgers, C. D., Davenport, Iowa

COMPANY D.

Becker, Phillip, Berkley, Iowa
Yount, E. J., Norwalk, Iowa
Yant, D., Spaulding, Iowa
Christy, W. D., Des Moines, Ia.
Painter, J. C., Des Moines, Iowa
Godfrey, G. L., Des Moines, Iowa
Husband, G. Y., Shell Rock, Iowa
Marsh, E. L., Des Moines, Iowa

COMPANY E.

Sims, W. S., Des Moines, Iowa
Moore, W. S., Des Moines, Iowa

COMPANY F.

Bateman, J. Y., Soldiers Home, Marshalltown, Iowa

COMPANY G.

Thorp, P. J., Beacon, Iowa
Moore, S. A., Bloomfield, Iowa

COMPANY H.

Amerine, Moses, Muscatine, Iowa
Varney, W. E., Wellman, Iowa
Corbin, S. L., West Liberty, Iowa

COMPANY K.

Cook, David, Oskaloosa, Iowa
Coyne, B., Richland, Kansas
Blake, Geo. W., Chariton, Iowa

7th IOWA INFANTRY.

Maj. Samuel M'Mahon, Ottumwa, Iowa.

COMPANY A.

Foulk, J. D., Marshalltown, Iowa
Morgan, Geo., Des Moines, Iowa

COMPANY B.

Trotter, J. A., Shell Rock, Iowa.

COMPANY C.

Snook, Isaiah, LaCelle, Iowa
Gaston, J. N., Boone County, Ia.
James, Barney, Union Mills, Ia.
Grant, James, Oskaloosa, Iowa
Baer, John R., Oskaloosa, Iowa
McDonough, J. P., Kirkville, Ia.
Martin, G. W., E. Des Moines, Iowa
Hoit, J. W., Albia, Iowa
Hoit, N., Ferry, Iowa
Mendenhall, G. W., New Sharon, Ia.
Phillips, Aaron, Lacey, Iowa
McDonough, L. C., Lacey, Iowa

COMPANY D.

Morrison, J. B., Ft. Madison, Ia. Francis, A. B., Oskaloosa, Iowa

COMPANY F.

Bearden, E. S., Newbern, Iowa Bartlett, U. S., Fremont, Iowa

COMPANY G.

Seaman, W. N., Des Moines, Ia. Fields, A. F., Colfax, Iowa
Laming, E. T., Marengo, Iowa Akers, J. W., Des Moines, Iowa
Kepner, R. Marengo, Iowa Burns, Robt., Newton, Iowa

COMPANY H.

Logan, S. M., Washington, Ia. Calhoun, S. S., Doblin, Iowa
Lewis, J. H., Nira, Iowa Glider, Geo., Wellman, Iowa
Rickey, C. D., Ottumwa, Iowa

COMPANY I.

Swanson, Mike, Knoxville, Iowa Swalm, C. P., Oskaloosa, Iowa

COMPANY K.

Spence, Tim, Knoxville, Iowa Morris, W., Springfield, Iowa
Horton, L., Richland, Iowa Gregory, Joel, Richland, Iowa
Rudolph, John, Keota, Iowa.

8TH IOWA INFANTRY.

Col. W. Bell, Washington, Iowa.

COMPANY A.

Smith, Spencer, Van Horn, Iowa Smith, P. A., Scranton, Iowa

COMPANY B.

Whitsel, J., Iowa City, Iowa

COMPANY C.

Carris, S. D., Doblin, Iowa Hall, R. N., Chicago, Illinois
Campbell, R. F., Keota, Iowa [539 Warren Ave.]
Prentiss, B. M., Bethany, Mo. Griffith, A. L., Des Moines, Iowa
Carl, J. H., Muscatine, Iowa Bill, W. B., Washington, Iowa
Currier, A. N., Iowa City, Iowa Bosworth, H. P., Clay, Iowa
Palmer, S. R., Dexter, Iowa

COMPANY D.

Harper, Alex, Vinton, Iowa Birch, Rollin D., Rockwell City, Ia.
Skea, J. P., Cedar Rapids, Iowa

COMPANY E.

McMillan, John, Knoxville, Iowa Jacob, Wm., Knoxville, Iowa
Neely, Joe, Flagler, Iowa Ryan, D., Newton, Iowa
Neely, Hen, Knoxville, Iowa Newman, Dave, Newbern, Iowa
Gaston, W., Knoxville, Iowa Kinkade, Len, Des Moines, Iowa
Roebuck, Wm. E., Attica, Iowa Banta, B. F., Knoxville, Iowa
Ryan, Robert, Lincoln, Nebraska Clark, A. M., Durham, Iowa
Curtis, H. G., Atlantic, Iowa

COMPANY F.

Kennon, J. C., Mt. Auburn, Iowa
Allen, D. E., Keswick, Iowa
Lamb, Daniel, Maxon, Iowa
Eaton, A. A., Atwood, Iowa
Carey, A. A., Des Moines, Iowa
Reynolds, W. E., Sigourney, Iowa
Perkins, G. W., Lacey, Iowa

COMPANY G.

Bush, W. P., Gilmore City, Iowa
Hedge, Jester, Montezuma, Iowa
Owen, G. W., Marengo, Iowa
Marshall, A., Carlisle, Iowa
Mentzer, J. B., Toddville, Iowa
Lyons, A. M., Marengo, Iowa
Eddy, W. M., Oxford, Iowa
Eddy, L., Oskaloosa, Iowa

COMPANY H.

Wells, Charles, Knoxville, Iowa
Ellis, F. M., Norwalk, Iowa
Sargent, W. W., Grinnell, Iowa
Blizzard, J. W., Ferry, Iowa
Zane, I. H., Oskaloosa, Iowa
Collin, E., Oskaloosa, Iowa
Dunlap, S. M., Des Moines, Iowa
Williams, C. T., Toledo, Iowa
McGlasson, W. T., Almina, Kan.
McFall, C. W., Orillia, Iowa
Kirkpatric, W. H., Oskaloosa, Ia.
Winder, W. W., Oskaloosa, Iowa

COMPANY I.

Turner, R. L., Oskaloosa, Iowa
Kahoa, Michael, Russell, Iowa
Adcock, L., Melrose, Iowa
Simmons, Jesse, Attica, Iowa
Turner, Asa, Oldfield, Iowa
Loevel, R. J., Woodburn, Iowa
Searle, C. P., Oskaloosa, Iowa

COMPANY K.

Graves, E., Juba, Illinois
Sullivan, J. B., Wapello, Iowa
Story, I. K., Indianola, Iowa
Humphrey, J. M., Greenfield, Iowa
Bartes, J. D., Marsh, Iowa
Moore, R. J. W., Cool, Iowa

12TH IOWA INFANTRY.

COMPANY A.

Cobb, G. H., Eldora Junction, Ia.
Wilson, T. H., Robertson, Iowa
Clarkson, Dick, Des Moines, Iowa
Sawin, G. S., Union, Iowa
Edgington, Capt. T. B., Memphis, Tennessee
Zieger, J. W., Eldora, Iowa

COMPANY C.

Reed, D. W., Pittsburg, Tenn.
Curtis, H. C., LeMars, Iowa

COMPANY D.

Soper, E. B., Emmetsburg, Iowa

COMPANY E.

Perry, A. B., Dunkerton, Iowa
Creighton David, Geneva, Iowa
Large, F. A., Laporte City, Iowa
Surfus, C. V., Bristow, Iowa

COMPANY F.

Stribling, C. C., Clifton, Tenn.
Tirrill, R. N., Manchester, Iowa
Dunham Abner, Manchester, Iowa

14th IOWA INFANTRY.

Shaw, Col. W. T., Anamosa, Iowa

COMPANY A.

Harvey, W., Killduff, Iowa
Hawfbaur, H., Buffalo, Iowa

COMPANY C.
Harmon, A. W., Sanborn, Iowa
Davidson, T. L., Searsboro, Iowa

COMPANY D.
Bishop, J. V., Springville, Iowa
Finley, J. H., Morning Sun, Iowa
Baldwin, T. T., Keokuk, Iowa

COMPANY E.
McGarah, J. D., Des Moines, Ia.
Cortney, J. J., Plymouth, Neb.
Horine, J. W., Swan, Iowa
Hodson, Wm., Vandalia, Iowa
Wegnor, August, Vandalia, Ia.
Brown, P. W., Runnels, Iowa
Johnson, R. H., Monroe, Iowa
Wallace, C., Vandalia
Murray, N., Vandalia, Iowa
Webb, Geo., Baxter, Iowa
Proner, Jacob, Fairmount, Iowa
Horn, G. H., Sheridan, Iowa

COMPANY F.
Gillott, J., Greenfield, Iowa
Eddy, A., Ross, Iowa
Hill, J., Exira, Iowa
Wheatly, R., Wilsonville, Iowa
Lengle, Jonathan, Oxford, Ia.
Douglas, J. E., Oxford, Iowa
Graham, Thos., Shueyville, Iowa
Carter, J., Sac City, Iowa

COMPANY G.
Clark, M., Laporte, Iowa
Mapolson, J., Reinbeck, Iowa
Haver, W. C., Winona, Minn

COMPANY H.
Birk, J., Anamosa, Iowa
Hartman, P., Anamosa, Iowa
Birk, A., Tipton, Iowa
Chapman, C., East Des Moines, Ia.
Drexler, J. C., Central City, Iowa

COMPANY I.
Savage, Joel, Middle River, Ia.
Clark, W. F., Marshalltown, Iowa

COMPANY K.
Dolbee, P. A., Bond, Kansas
Dolbee, E. M., Bond, Kansas
Thompson, W. H., Medeapolis, Ia.
Barton, M. V., Russell, Iowa
Lewis, A. K., Arlington, Neb.
Bowen, Jas. A., Subte, Missouri
Storks, W. D., Oakville, Iowa
Watson, J. D., Kossuth, Iowa
McMakin, W. T., Middletown, Ia.
Campbell, W. J., Elrick, Iowa
Chapman, Samuel, Plattsmouth, Neb.

NOTICE TO COMRADES.

We kindly ask all the comrades who receive this pamphlet to send 25 cents to help defray expense of publication. The money will be placed in the hands of the treasurer. This seems a small matter, but if you will do this, the burden will fall on all, and the expense will be easily met. Send to R. L. TURNER.

315, 3d Av. East, Oskaloosa, Iowa.

www.ingramcontent.com/pod-product-compliance
Lightning Source LLC
Chambersburg PA
CBHW031609110426
42742CB00037B/1383